I0214229

# Volume 04
## Visualizing Architecture

Alex Hogrefe

# Volume 04
## Visualizing Architecture

**www.visualizingarchitecture.com**

Copyright © 2016 Alex Hogrefe

All rights reserved. This book or any portion thereof
may not be reproduced or used in any manner
whatsoever without the expressed written permission
of the publisher except for the use of brief quotations
in a book review.

ISBN 978-0-9913829-3-4

# Porttg

olio

Center

ts

**Preface
2016**

This portfolio is an exploration in architectural graphic representation. Each of the four projects are designed across a spectrum of conditions; from urban to rural settings and landscapes to buildings. Each of the investigations are intended to act as a framework to test out new graphic ideas and styles. They are not designed for clients, nor are they intended to be built.

The book is conceived around experimentation and exploration. Each spread investigates representation through an intentionally different lens. Though the styles range, each spread has been carefully composed and certain organizational systems have been deployed to unify the layouts and create a consistency throughout the book.

With each image, I use a limited palette of software, using each tool for its specific capabilities. For my work, I use Sketchup as the modeler, V-Ray for rendering, AutoCAD for line work, and Photoshop for post processing and page layout. This combination of tools allows a greater flexibility throughout the work and gives the right balance of speed and simplicity. As technology and software develop new interfaces and methods, my technical workflow also evolves.

At the end of this portfolio, an image index breaks down all of the images to reveal the process images used to generate the final illustration. Many of the processes and workflows used in the making of this book are also broken down into simplified tutorials. These tutorials and other information can be found on my website:

**www.visualizingarchitecture.com**

A special thank you to my wife, Kim, as well as Jeff Kruth and Matt Uminski.

# Abou

this....

t
his

This

# LONG WHARF
# REINVENTED

**Project:** Wharf Ticketing, Bar, and Museum
**Location:** Boston, Massachusetts, USA
**Date:** August 16, 2014

01

In 1710, the Boston Long Wharf was constructed as a major shipping center extending nearly a half-mile. Over time, much of the wharf was reclaimed for public activities that are now popular tourist destinations such as Quincy Market and the Boston Greenway. Today, the Wharf primarily acts as a hub for harbor cruises, ferries, and views towards the harbor. Despite numerous activities and destinations, a cohesive fabric and identity along the water remains elusive. Scattered tourist destinations and multiple developments create an incomplete urban procession. By rethinking the programmatic configuration and adjusting the form, the wharf can clarify its place in the city as a destination point rather than a place visitors pass through. A better reconfiguration can take on the dual purpose of telling the story of its past as well as becoming the ideal destination to view the harbor activity.

North End Gateway

City Hall

Quincy Market

Long Wharf

Aquarium

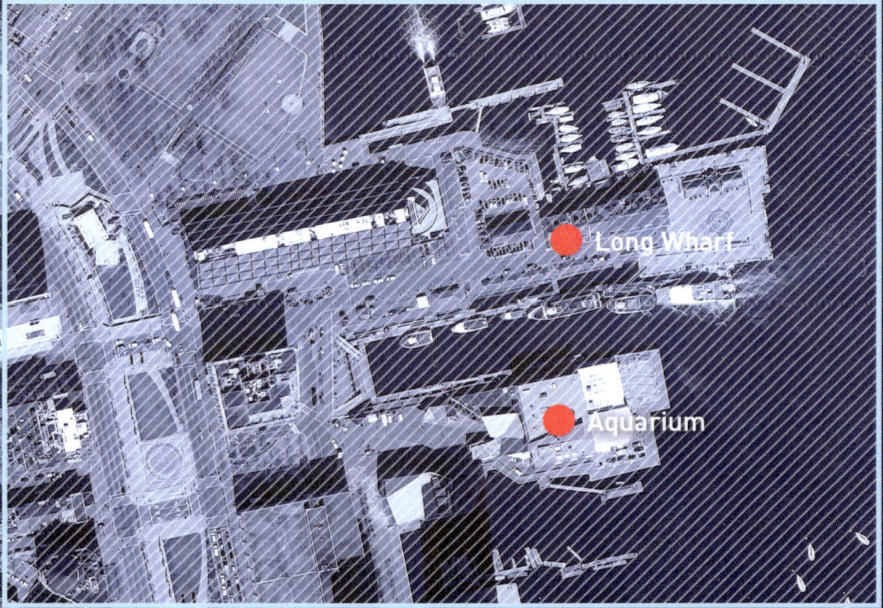

## Site Complexity Breakdown

The wharf sits adjacent to one of the greatest American urban processions with multiple focal points. Pedestrian traffic flows from the City Hall Plaza into Quincy Market, across the greenway, and into Long Wharf. Much of the pedestrian traffic is focused towards the landside of the wharf where tourists visit pavilions and can board harbor cruises and ferries. Some visitors continue to the end of the wharf to lookout over the harbor. However, a lack of amenities that heighten the historical and contemporary connections means limited engagement with the site and its surroundings. Rather than a grand sequence terminating in a grand finale, visitors instead quickly move on.

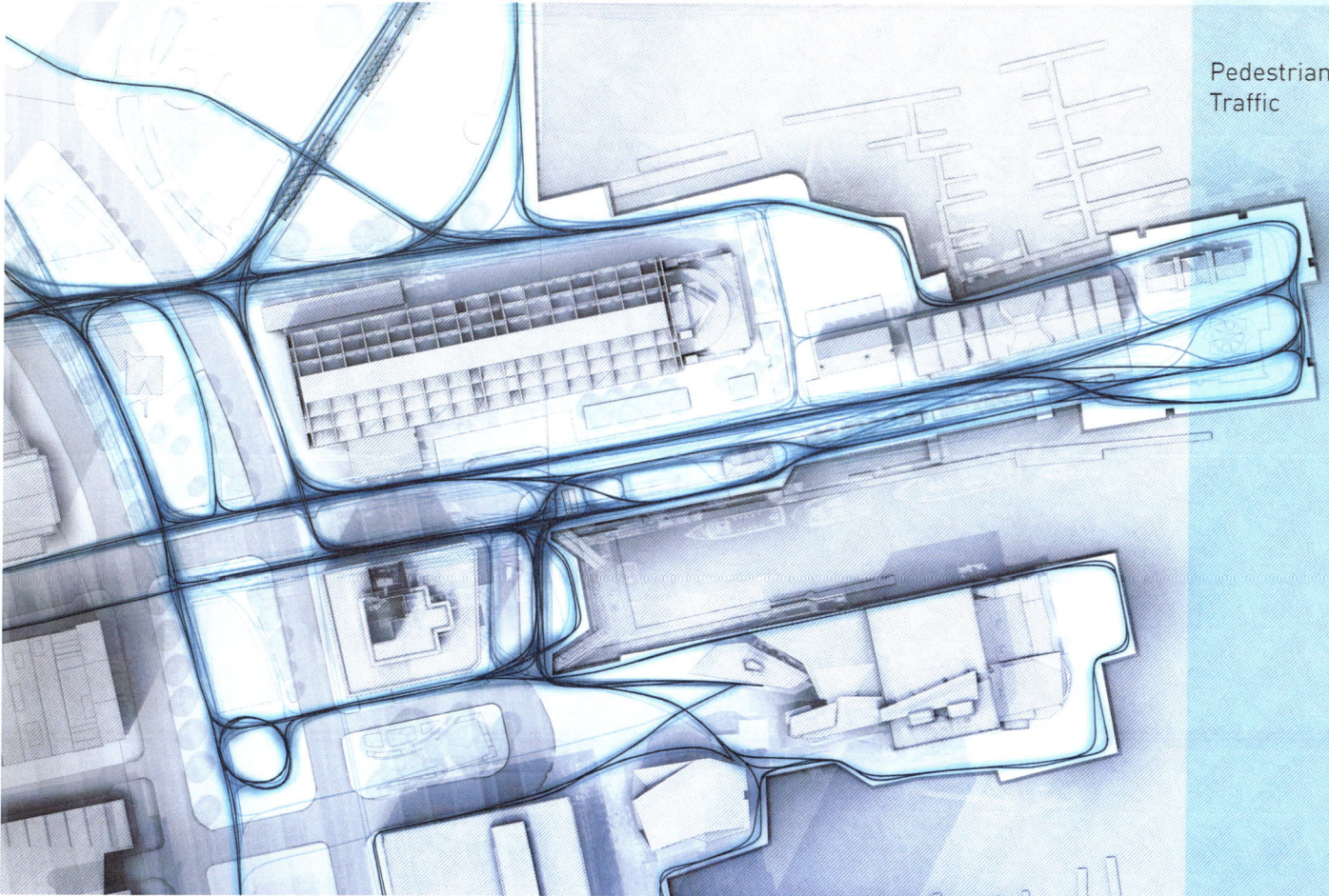

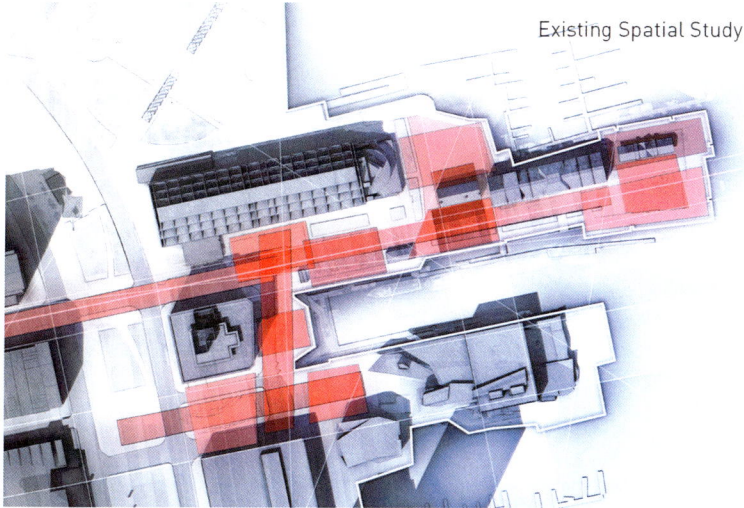

Existing Spatial Study

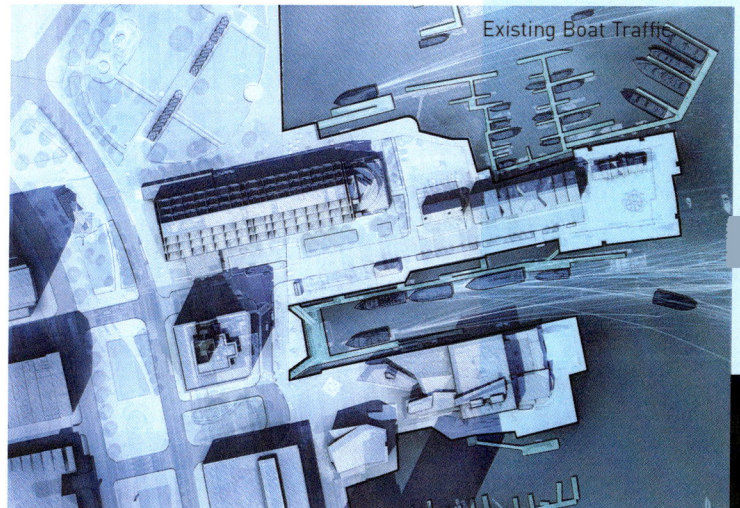

Existing Boat Traffic

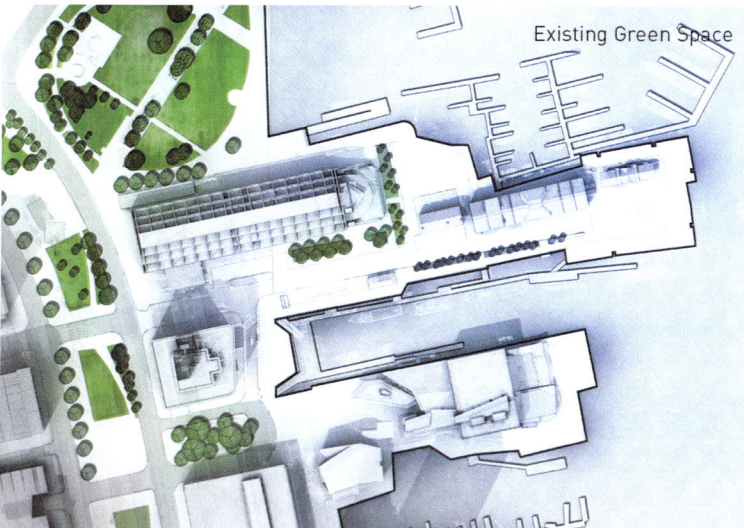

Existing Green Space

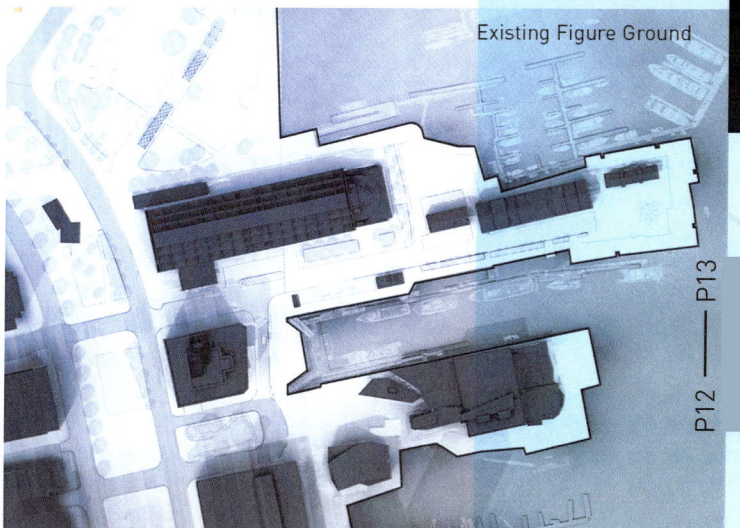

Existing Figure Ground

## Existing Site

The current wharf lacks organization and pedestrian flow. Minimal seating means most visitors can only stay for short periods of time before moving on to the next location. The wharf is not seen as a destination, but instead as a short stop on a path.

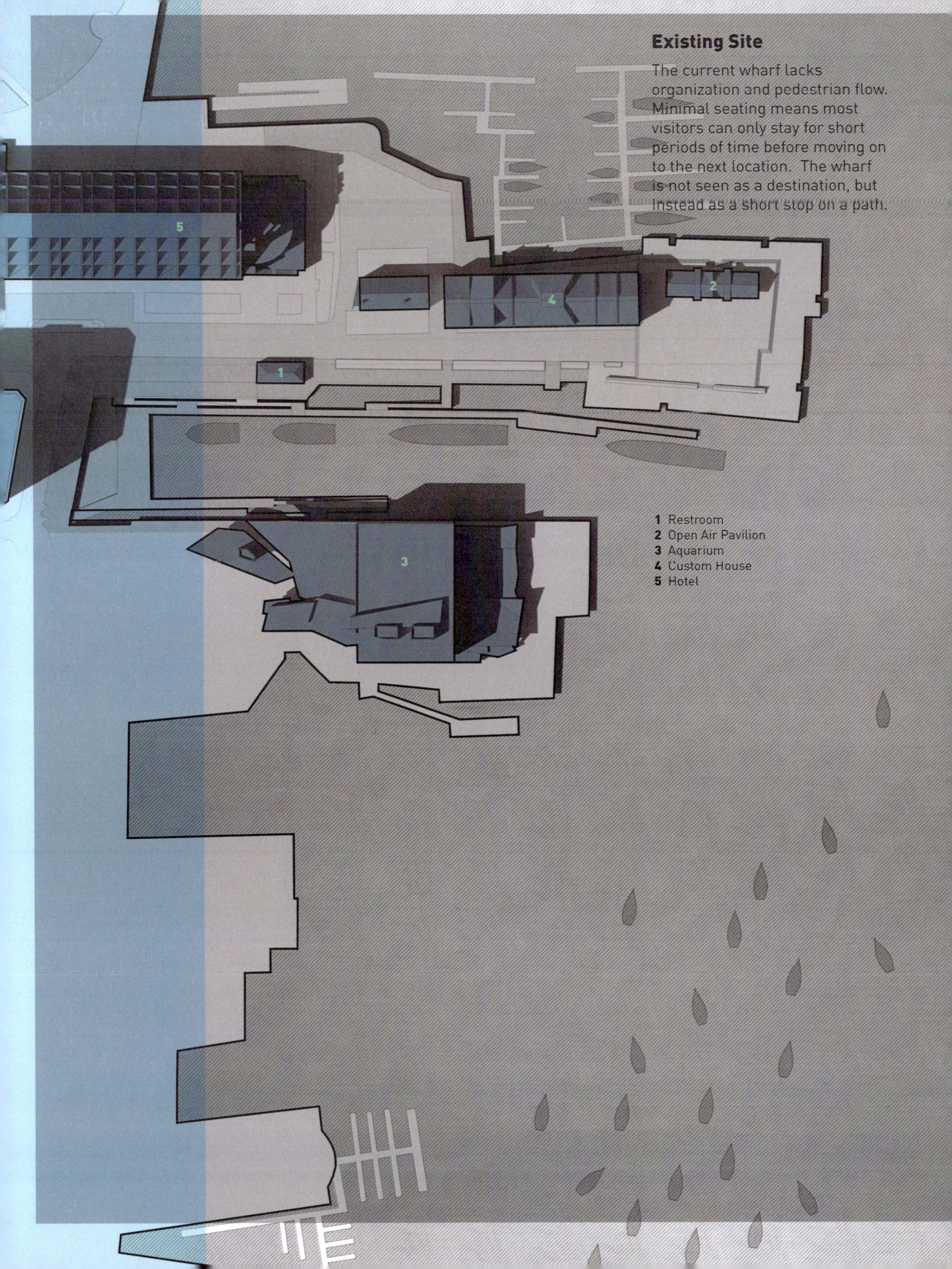

5

4

2

1

3

**1** Restroom
**2** Open Air Pavilion
**3** Aquarium
**4** Custom House
**5** Hotel

## Proposed Design

The new wharf design reorganizes the program to work with pedestrian traffic and introduces new points of interest including a museum and tiered seating. This encourages visitors to slow down and explore the site.

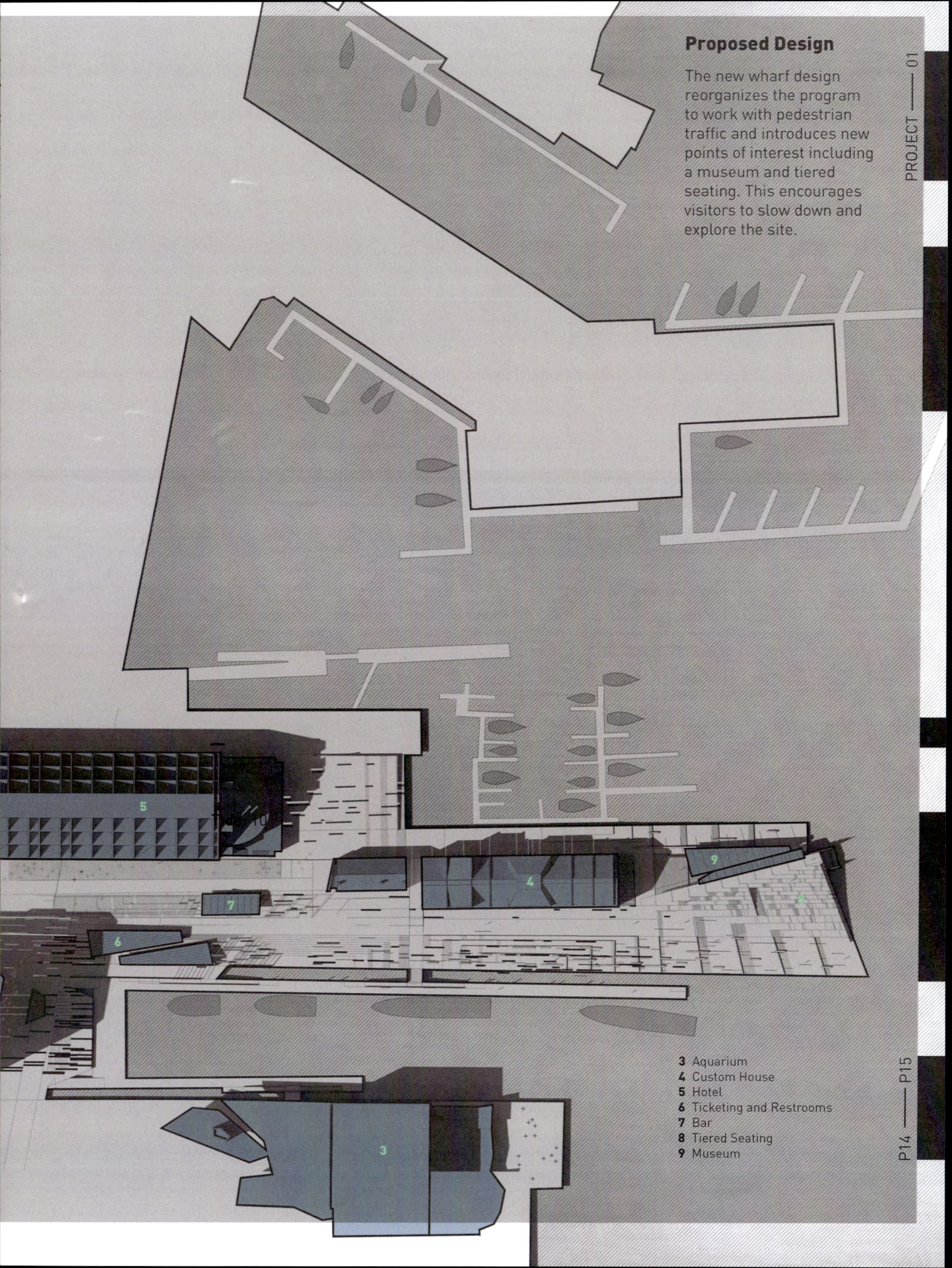

3 Aquarium
4 Custom House
5 Hotel
6 Ticketing and Restrooms
7 Bar
8 Tiered Seating
9 Museum

Block Seating

Embedded Lighting

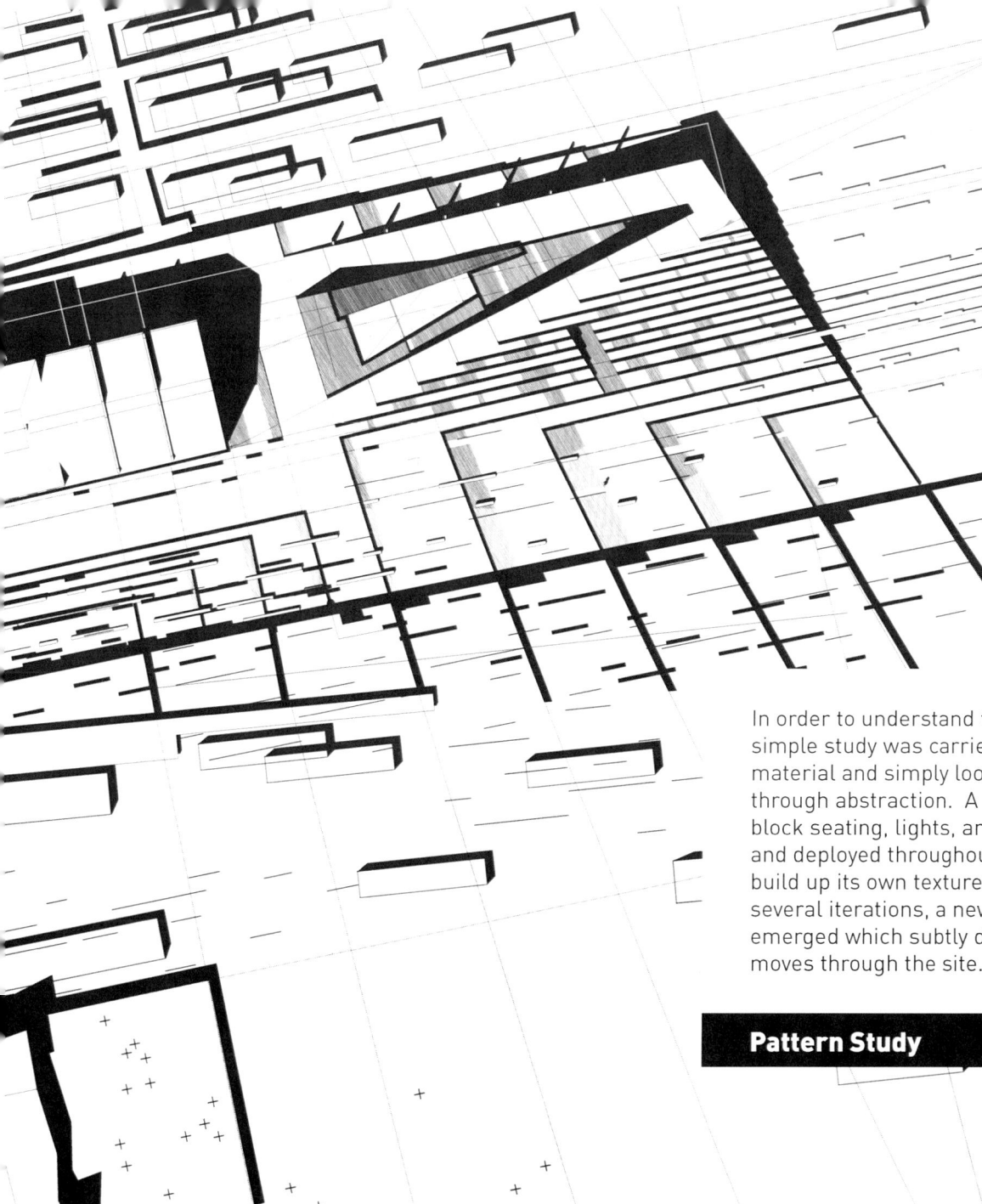

| | Boats/ Ferries |
| | Material Change |
| | Light Strips |
| | Block Seating |
| | Level Change |

In order to understand the complexities of the site, a simple study was carried out that removed color and material and simply looked at ground plane elements through abstraction. A lexicon of elements such as block seating, lights, and level change were created and deployed throughout the site in such a way as to build up its own texture on a macro scale. Through several iterations, a new language of site textures emerged which subtly define unique spaces as one moves through the site.

## Pattern Study

Level Change

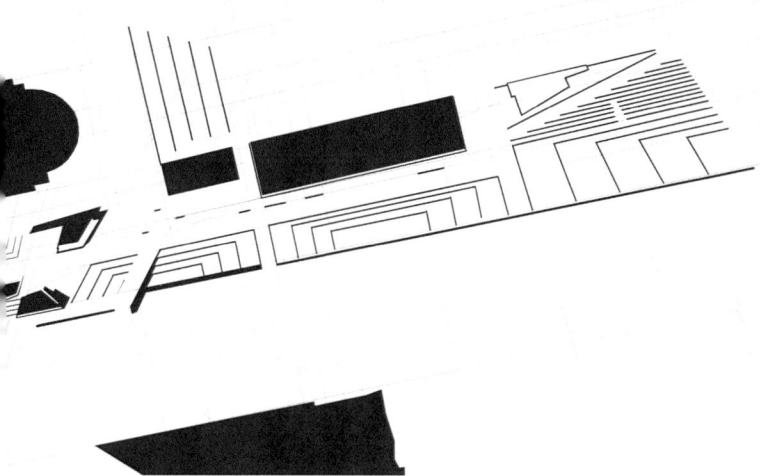

Material Change

## Historic Long Wharf Extension

The original wharf stretched nearly a half a mile inland when it was originally built. Infill over the years left little of the original wharf intact. However, a strong visual axis still remains, creating a connection through to the Old State House. An opportunity exists to acknowledge the historic long wharf through material and texture activating State Street into a vibrant promenade.

Old State House

Quincy Market

R.K. Greenway

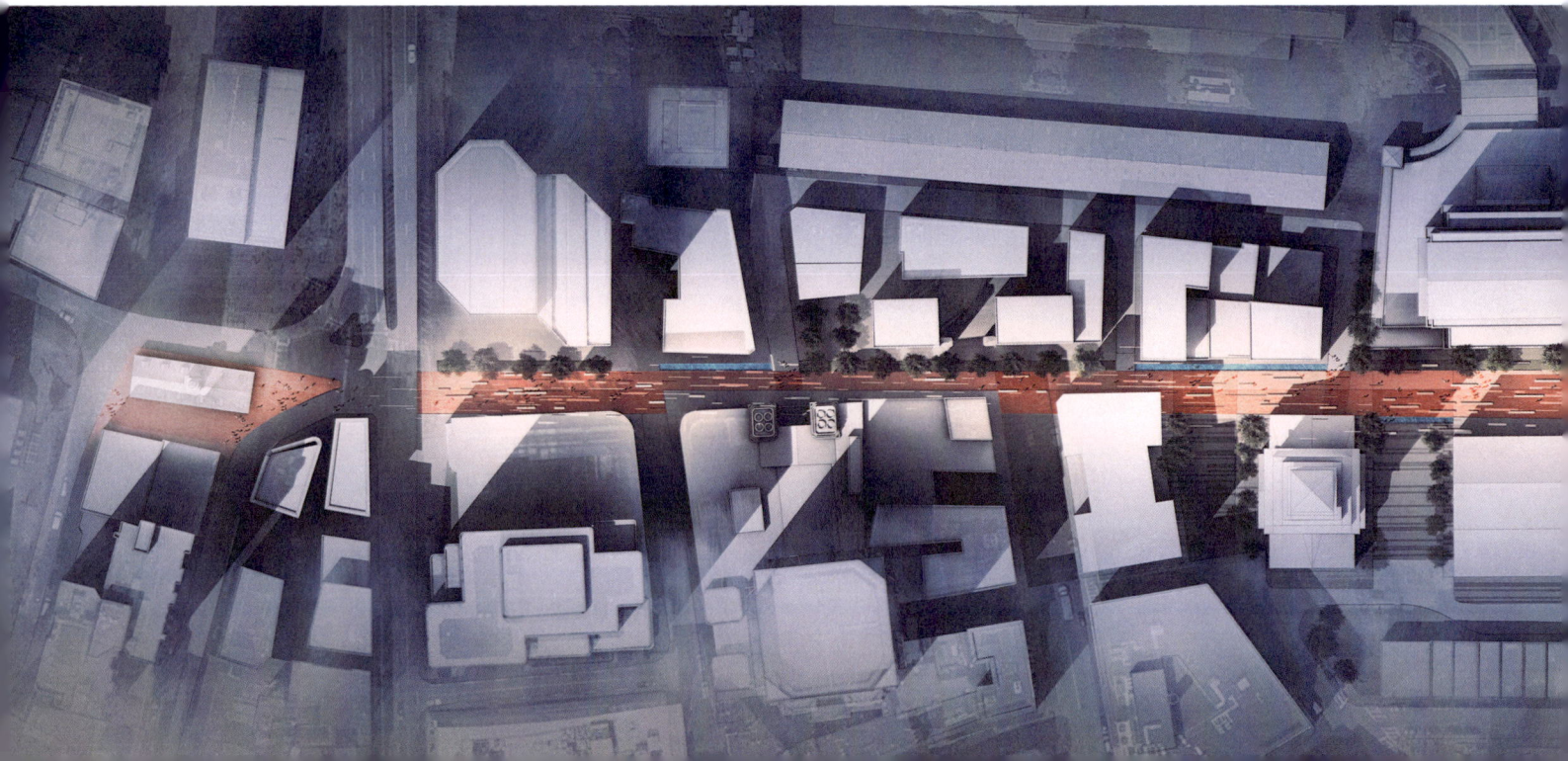

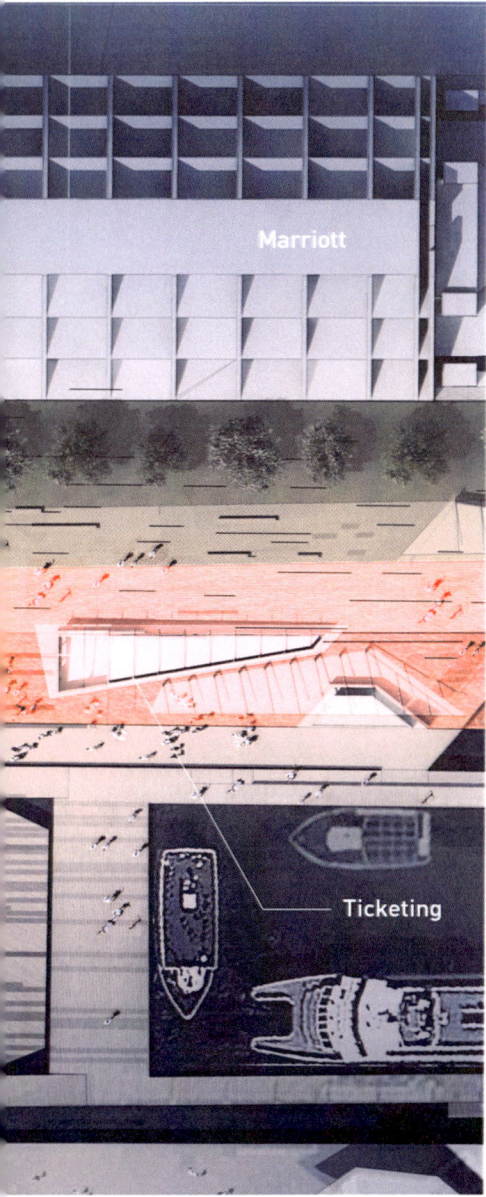

Marriott

Ticketing

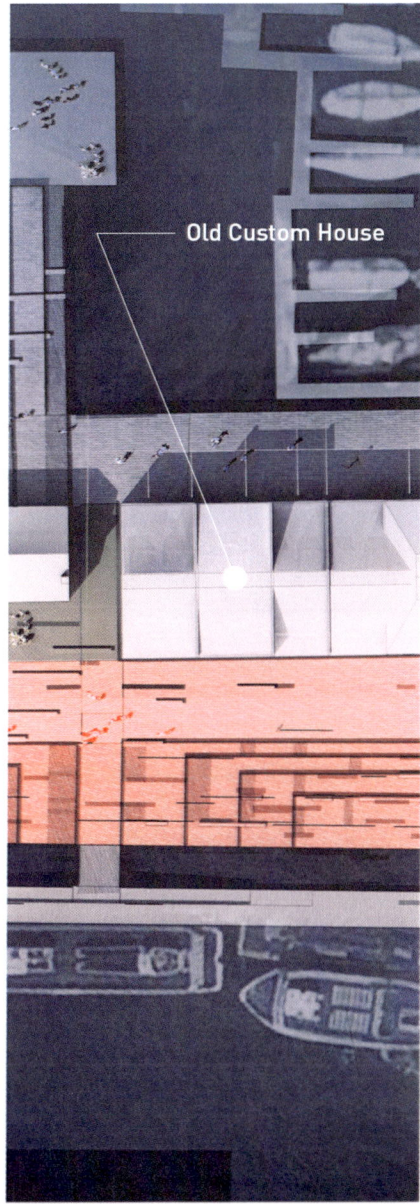

Old Custom House

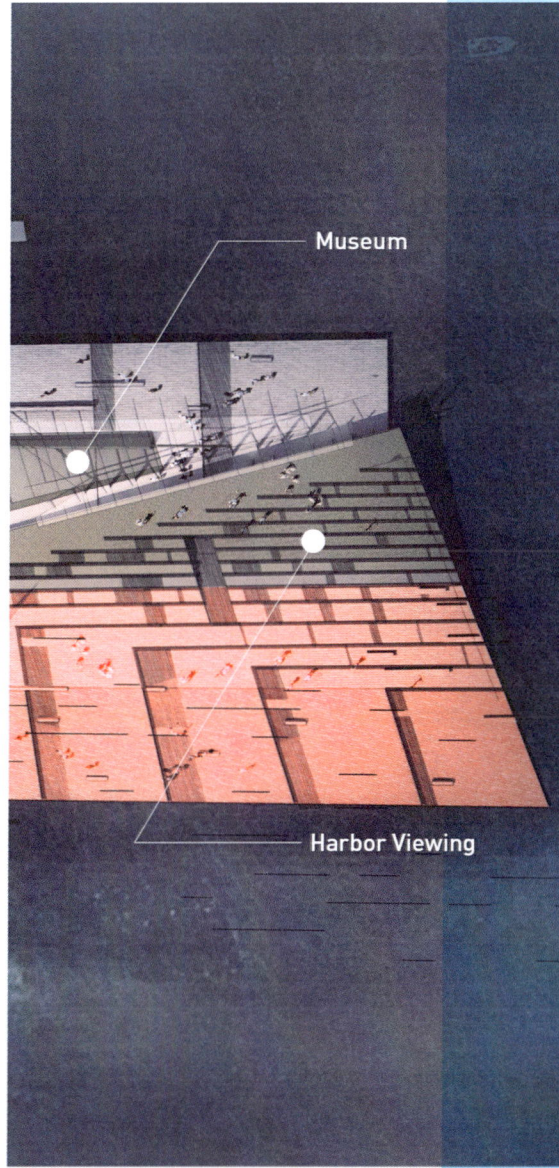

Museum

Harbor Viewing

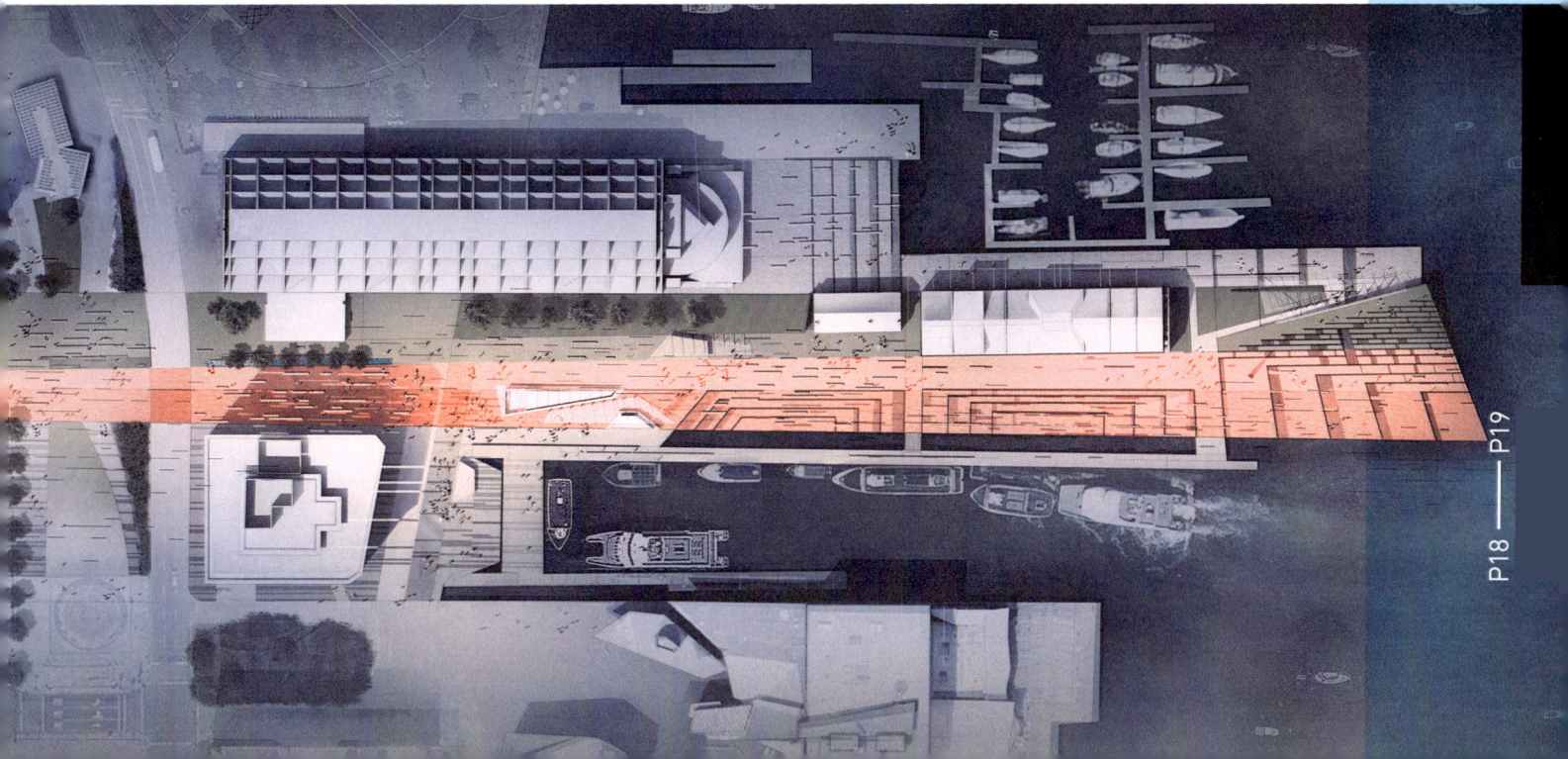

## Tide Morphology

The wharf is sculpted through multiple tiers
responding to changing tide levels. As the tide begins
to reach its highest points, parts of the decking
submerge changing the floor plan of the wharf. The
wharf then intimately interacts with the Boston Harbor
through tactile and changing temporal experiences.

Tide: 7'

Tide: 9'

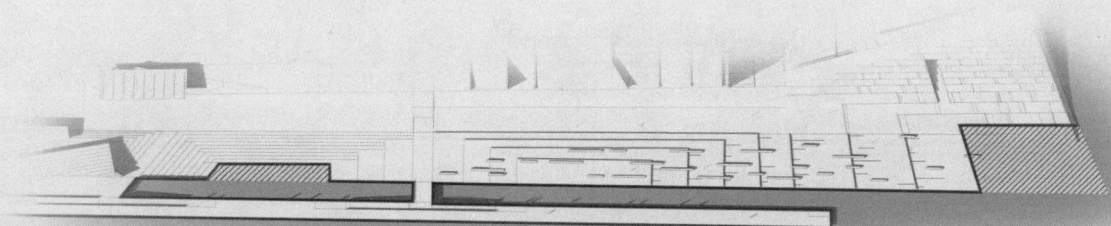

Tide: 10'

## Harbor Vessel Viewing

The Long Wharf Redevelopment brings emphasis back to the harbor and the vistas that it creates. One of Boston's greatest assets is put on display by introducing a simple yet defined viewing grandstand. Visitors can view the touring vessels and ferries coming in and out of the harbor from a variety of locations. Each zone of the wharf creates unique viewing experiences allowing everyone to find their perfect spot.

# The Harbor Lantern

The wharf now acts as a lantern at the end of a historic axis. The wharf stays active through the integration of light and activities.

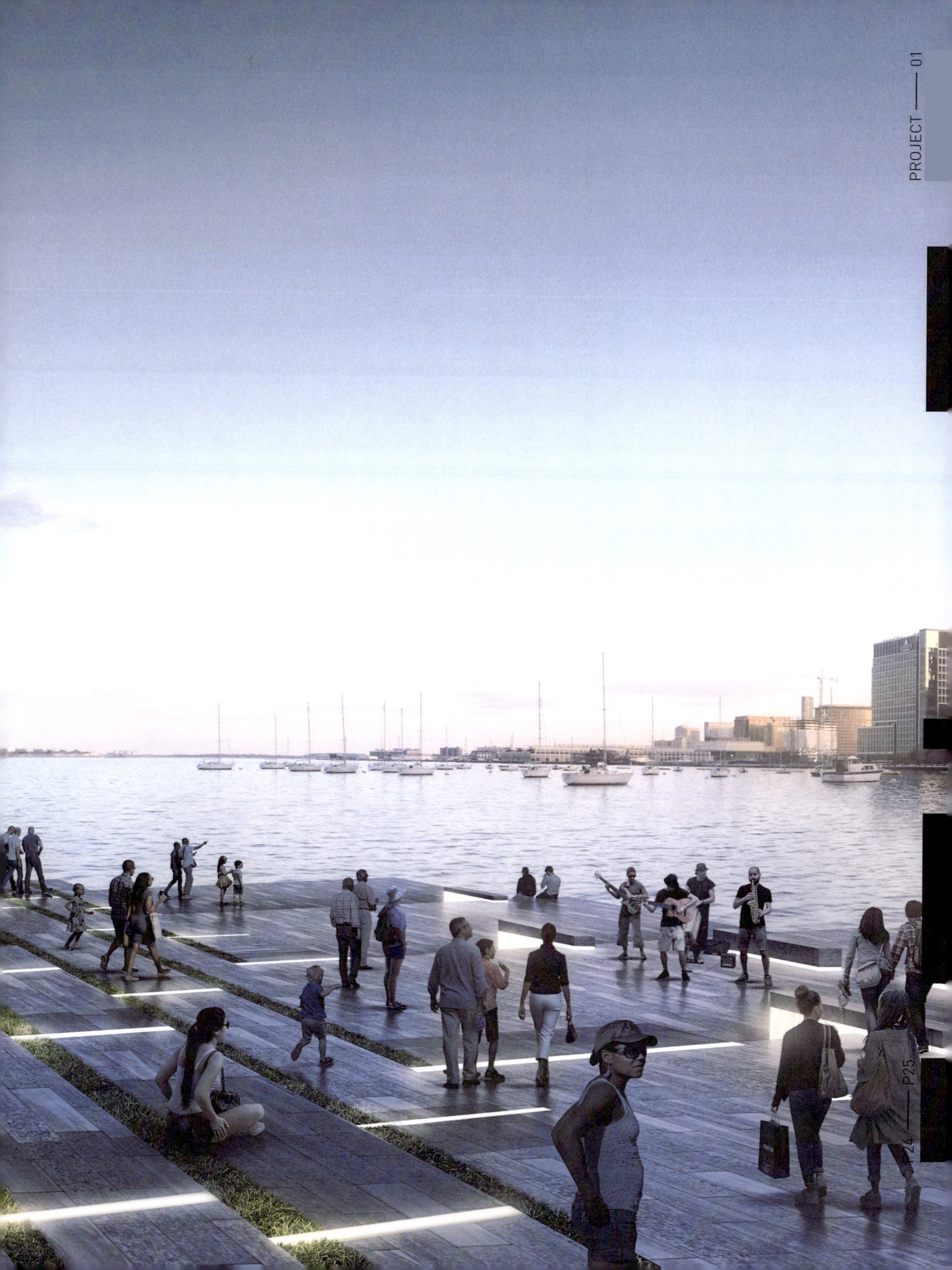

# CULTURAL
# CENTER

| | |
|---|---|
| **Project:** | Office, Exhibition, and Educational Space |
| **Location:** | Boston, Massachusetts, USA |
| **Date:** | January 02, 2014 |

## 02

Boston is home to a multi-faceted cultural scene. Through its layered history, educational centers, and continued economic importance, a unique cultural scene persists. Museums, theaters, and libraries are dense throughout the city. The design for a new Cultural Center creates a place for both tourists and residents to come together to learn, discuss, create, and promote the unique culture of Boston. This project sits adjacent to the Rose Fitzgerald Kennedy Greenway and proposes a structure that activates a quiet corner adjacent to some of Boston's most popular destinations. Through its strategic placement, the Cultural Center creates a new point of interest encouraging people to explore beyond the traditional flow of traffic.

**Boston, MA**

North End
Gateway

Quincy Market

City Hall

1100'

Long Wharf

Aquarium

800'

Rose
Kennedy
Greenway

0'    100'  200'    400'      600'

John Fitzgerald Surface Rd.

Milk St.

Atlantic Ave.

India St.

India St.

Broad St.

## Edges and Axes

The site is in close proximity to some of Boston's most iconic destinations. Though they are not directly visible from the chosen site, they are connected by popular pedestrian paths through the Rose Kennedy Greenway. The design is sculpted to provide views through and around the nearby context while still relating to the existing city grid and holding the street edge of John Fitzgerald Surface Road.

0'  20'  50'      100'              200'

### Site

The form of the design is largely influenced by the trapezoidal shape of the site and surrounding site forces. The design conforms to the extents of the site to maximize area.

### Plinth

A base is extruded to create amphitheater seating and commercial retail at the ground level.

### Vertical Circulation

Vertical circulation is placed in two different locations to access the floating upper levels and creates both a public and private entry.

### Horizontal Circulation

Horizontal circulation is wide
and meandering providing
opportunities for exhibition space.

### Program

The use of the Cultural Center is
broken into three zones physically
defined by the massing: office
space, educational space, and
exhibition space.

### Glazing/Screens

In order to frame views and
manage privacy, glazing and
screens are strategically
deployed.

## Attracting and Repelling

Through plan, the Cultural Center responds to the surrounding context both through form and material. The massing splits and shifts to acknowledge the streets and scale of the nearby buildings. A new material palette is introduced including steel and wood, but retains color tonality to the existing fabric. This reaction to the context sets up a theme of awareness of the city that will be continued through exhibits inside the space.

## Street Engagement

The Cultural Center dynamically responds to engage the public realm by shifting to meet the greenway and surrounding blocks. A large plinth is inserted and is molded to generate different public spaces. Facing the park, a grand stair doubles as tiered seating. Parts of the plinth are carved out to make space for cafes and retail below. At night, the large programmatic volumes are lit from below acting as a beacon and inviting visitor in even in the worst of the weather.

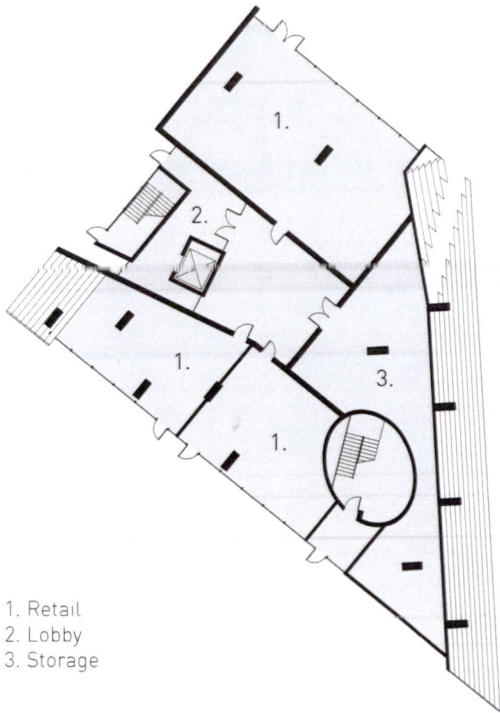

1. Retail
2. Lobby
3. Storage

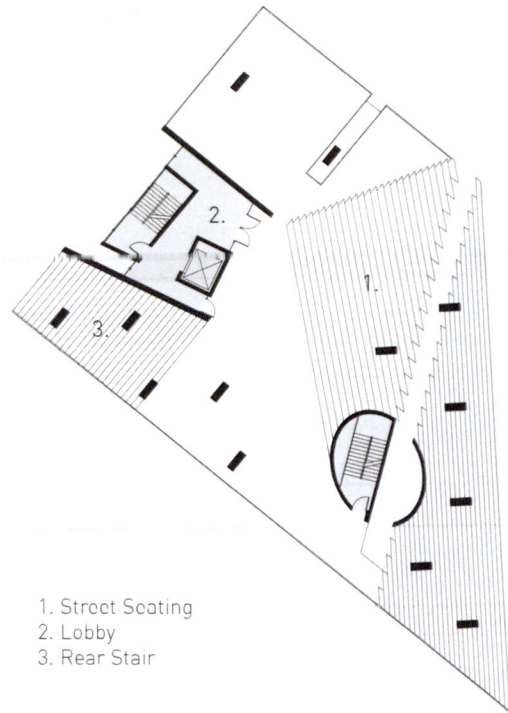

1. Street Seating
2. Lobby
3. Rear Stair

EQ-A    EQ-B        EQ-B        EQ-A

12'

18'

12'

12'

12'

12'

12'

7'

18'

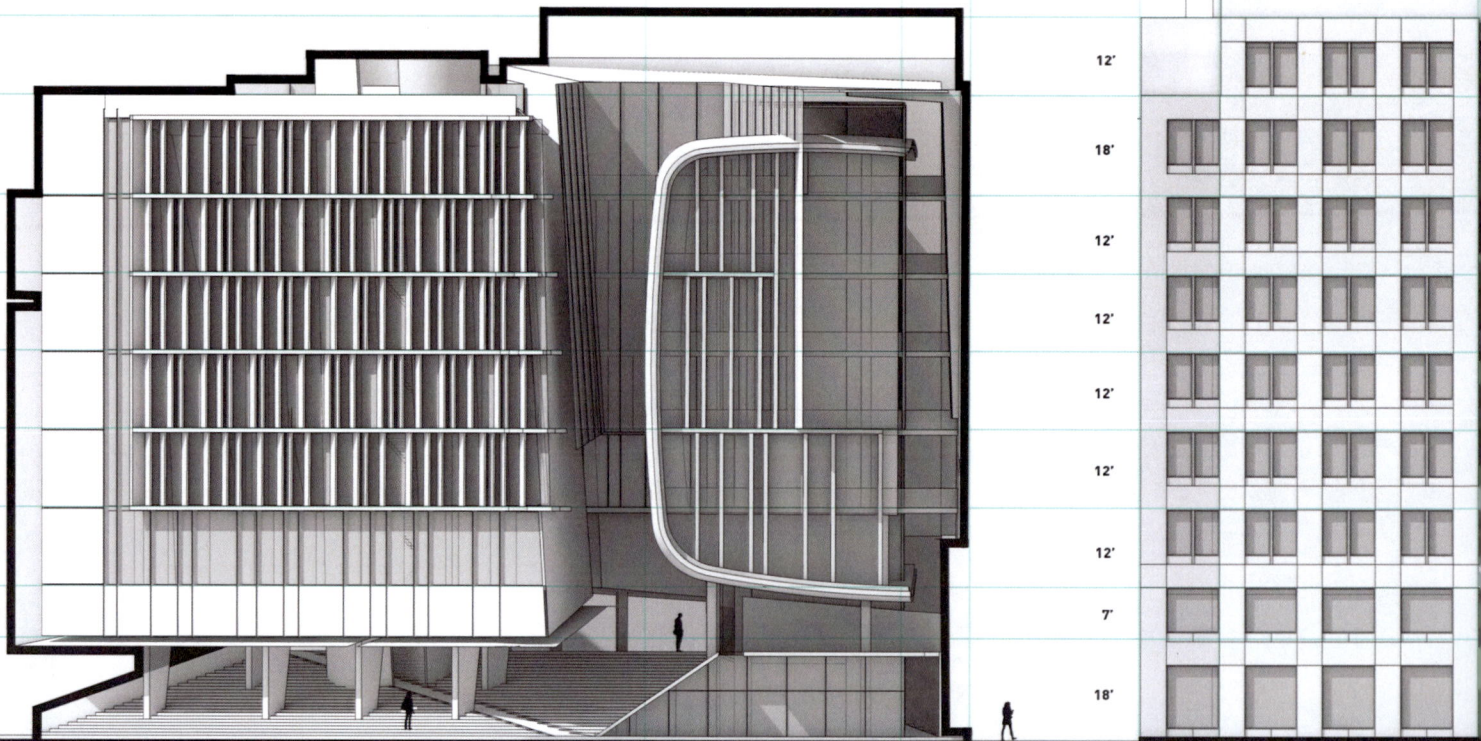

**North Elevation**

1. Lecture
2. Conf. Rm.
3. Office Suite
4. Exhibition
5. Balcony

1. Roof Garden
2. Mechanical
3. Exhibition

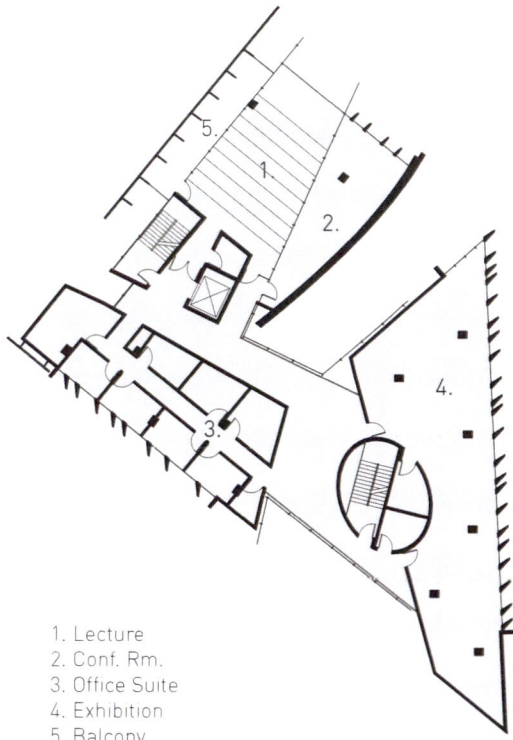

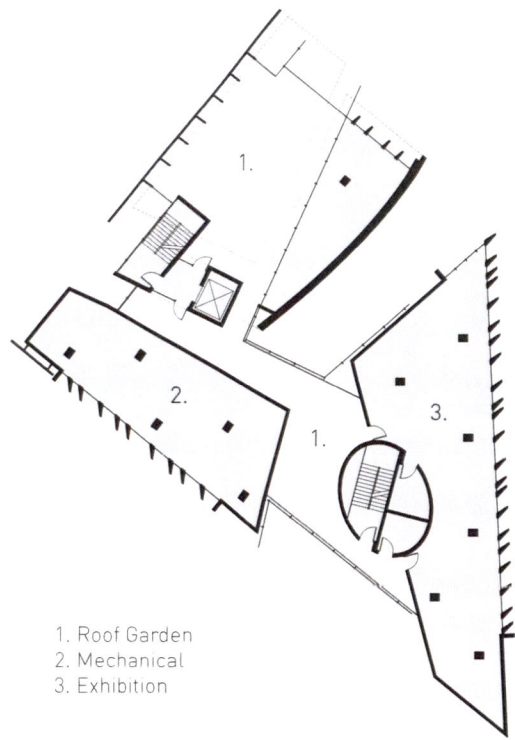

**4th Floor Plan**

EQ-A          EQ-B

**Roof Plan**

EQ-A          EQ-B

18'

12'

12'

12'

12'

12'

12'

6'

18'

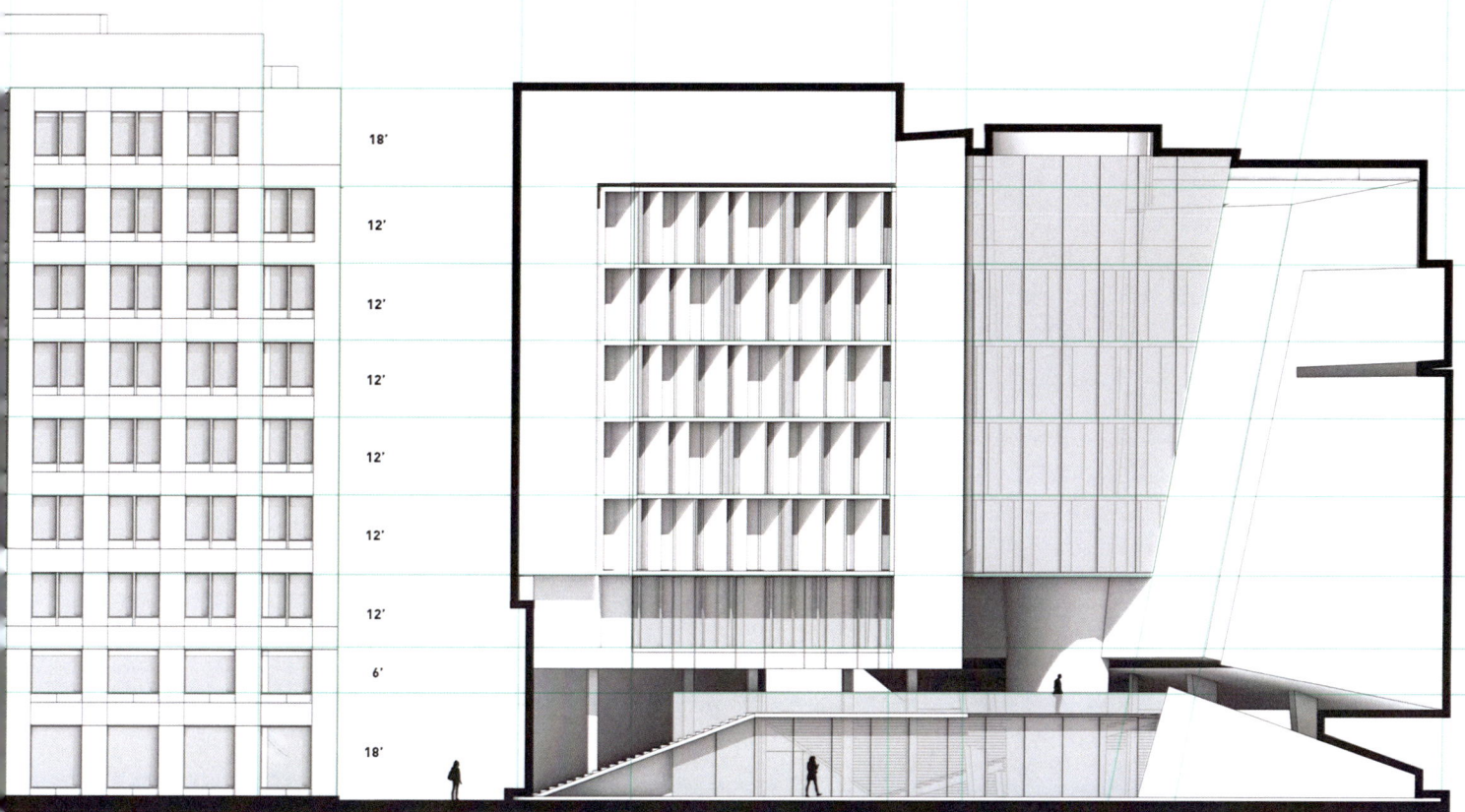

**South Elevation**

## City Anchor

The Cultural Center design attempts to provide a place where culture, art, and architecture can promote and nurture a new generation of growth that reflects its city's values. It is a place for connecting, learning, and sharing ideas to ensure a living dialog continues across the community.

**Project:** Train Viewing Platform, Hotel, and Museum
**Location:** Deshler, Ohio, USA
**Date:** September 14, 2015

# 03

Deshler is a small rural village of 4,000 residents located in Northwest, Ohio. At the town's crossroads, visual follies - the coal chute, water tower, and rail passenger station - tie together the surrounding historic fabric. However, many of these historic structures are decommissioned and have fallen into disrepair. Lately, Deshler has seen a new revitalization through heritage tourism. The village has become a hub for trainspotting where railroad enthusiasts come from around the country to view engines roar through town. This project looks to take advantage of this new trend to rebuild the town's identity and offer a new source of Main Street revitalization.

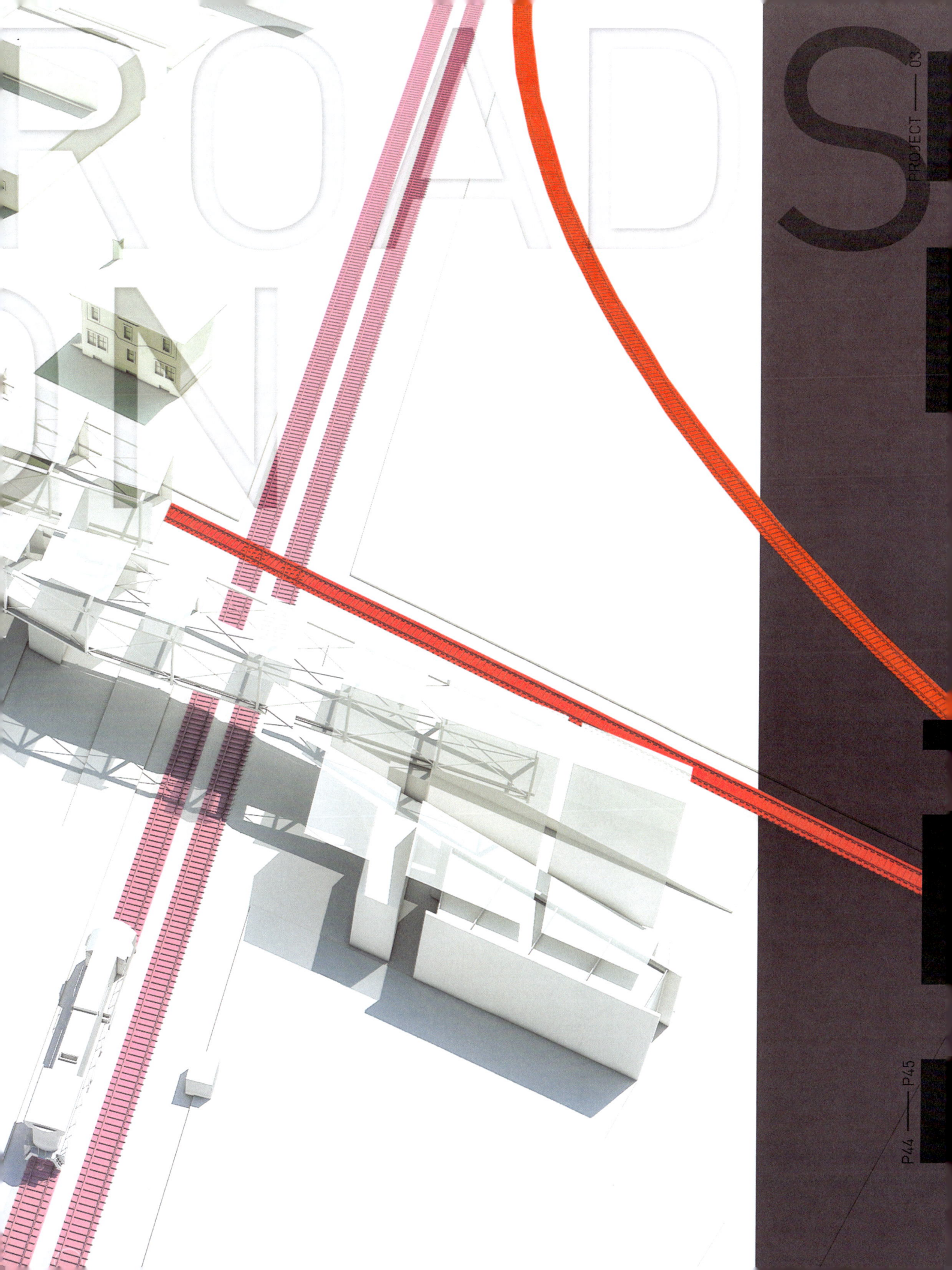

Grain Elevator

Main Street

2

Railroad Tracks

Site

18

Railroad Tracks

1

Reservoirs

Water Tower

0'      75'      150'                          300'

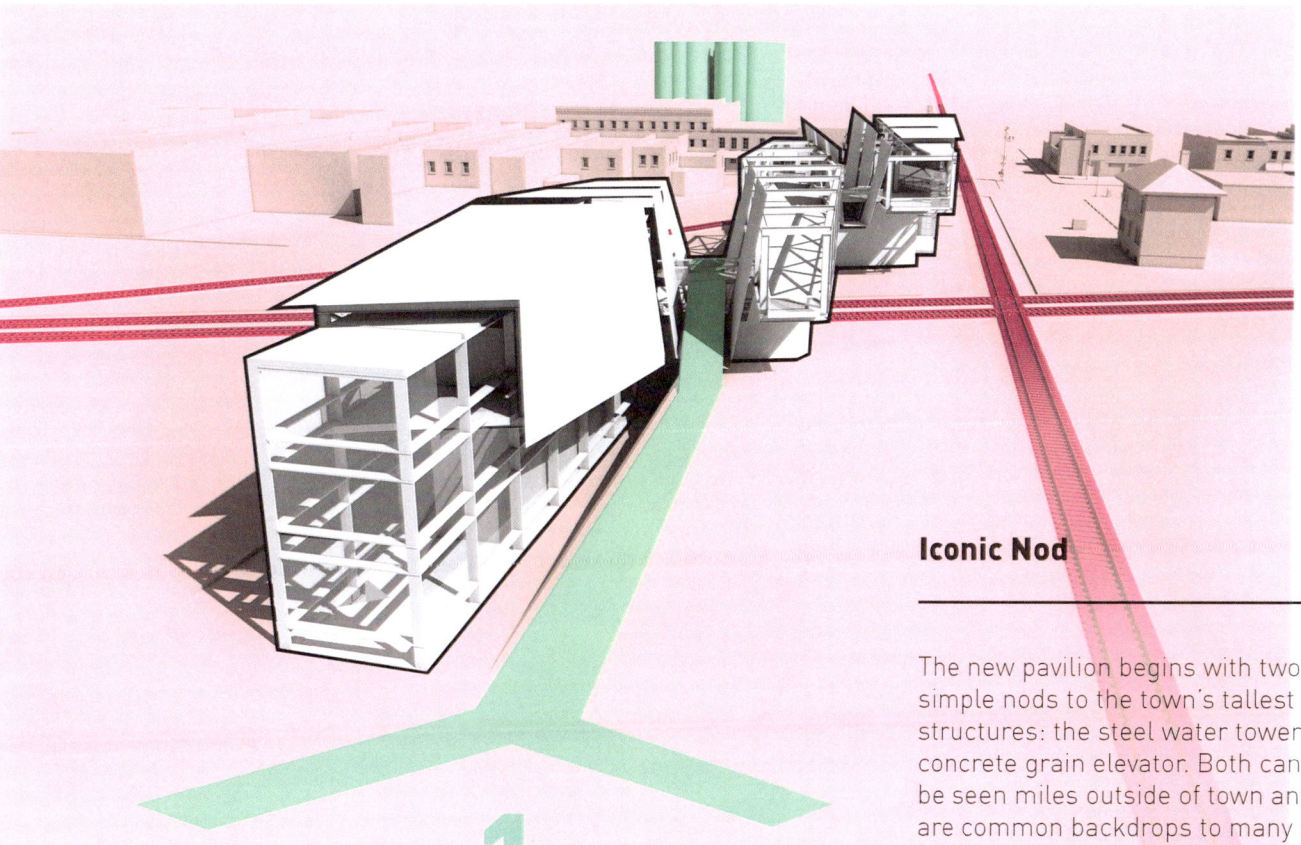

**1** Axis Looking North

## Iconic Nod

The new pavilion begins with two simple nods to the town's tallest structures: the steel water tower and concrete grain elevator. Both can be seen miles outside of town and are common backdrops to many of the train photos taken on site. The pavilion design deforms on both sides of the east and west running tracks providing a framed view of these iconic structures as pedestrians ascend the ramps to the viewing bridge.

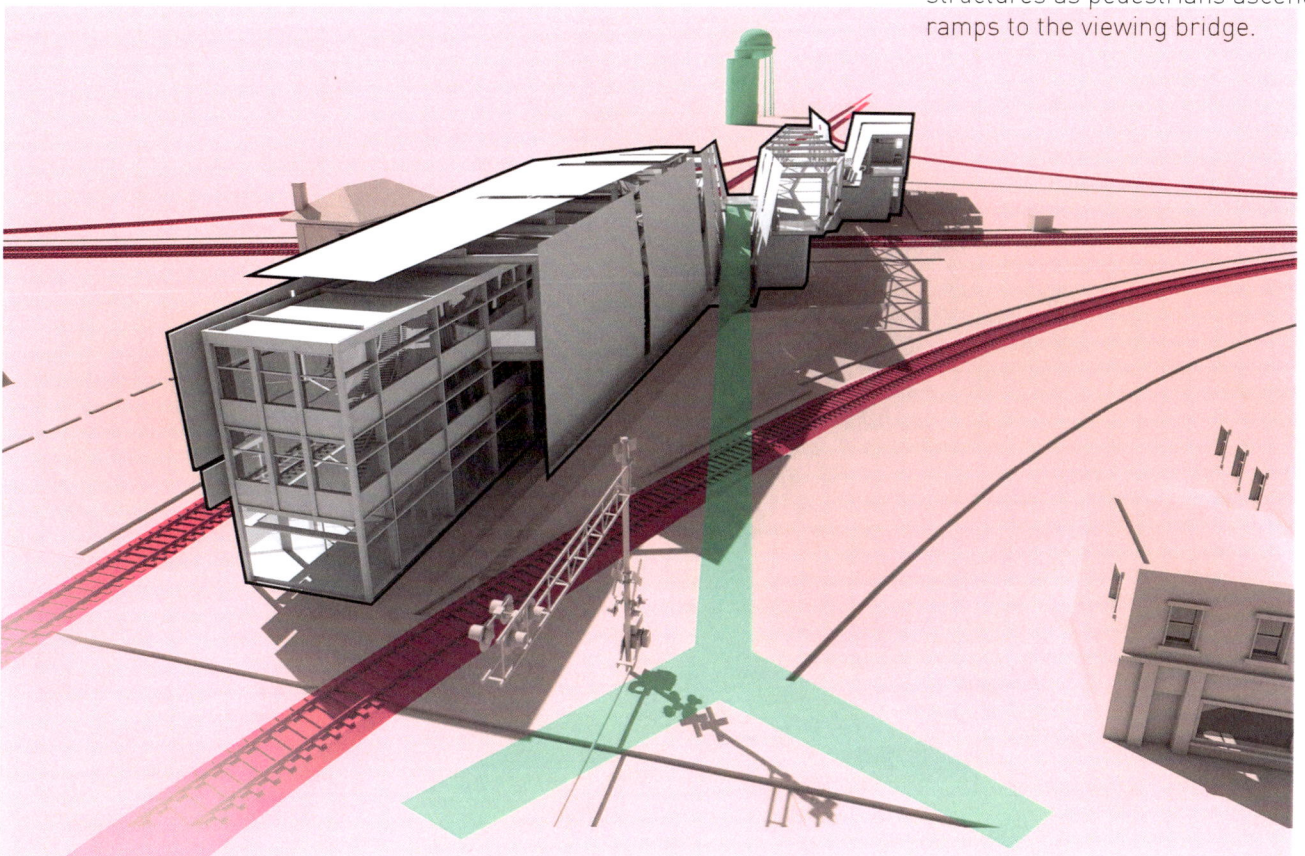

**2** Axis Looking South

## View South

The view south can be considered the most scenic of the views, framed by the town water towers and reservoirs. Visitors gain a unique view of approaching trains as they dine at the upper cafe. Part of the floor is glazed to allow view of the trains as they pass by.

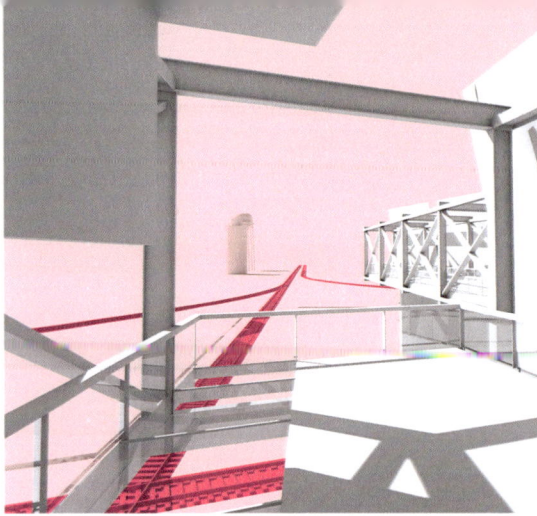

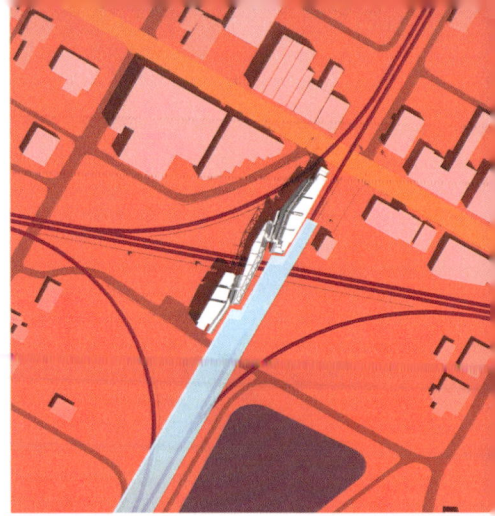

## View West

Standing on the bridge, guests can watch trains from a unique perspective. The town's density is lower in this direction. Few trees impede the view meaning trains can be seen approaching from miles away.

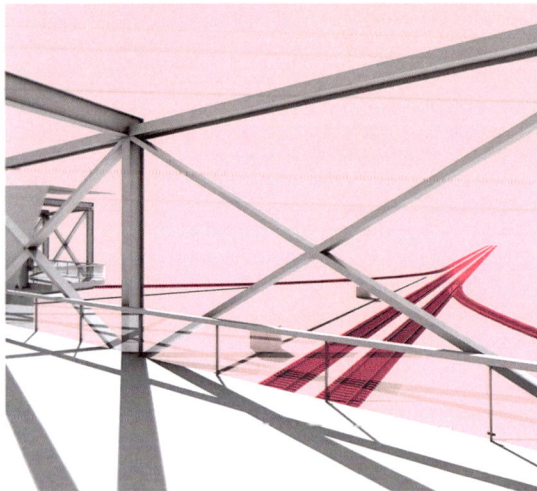

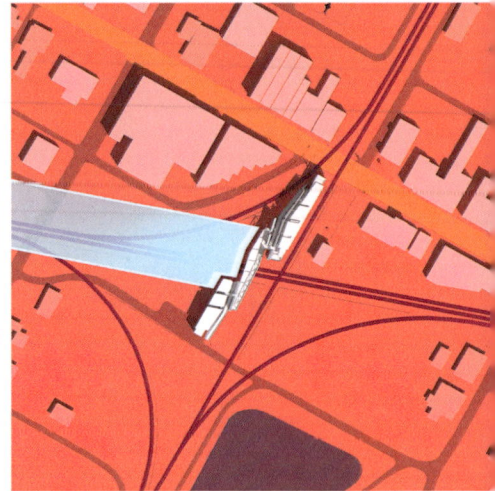

## View North

The north view looks over Main Street and is framed by the grain elevators just beyond. The town is at its highest density in this direction with the alfalfa mill and baseball fields seen in the distance.

## View East

Looking east, visitors can see the town post office, old lumber mill, and fire station. The hotel rooms face to the east and sit parallel to the north/south running tracks.

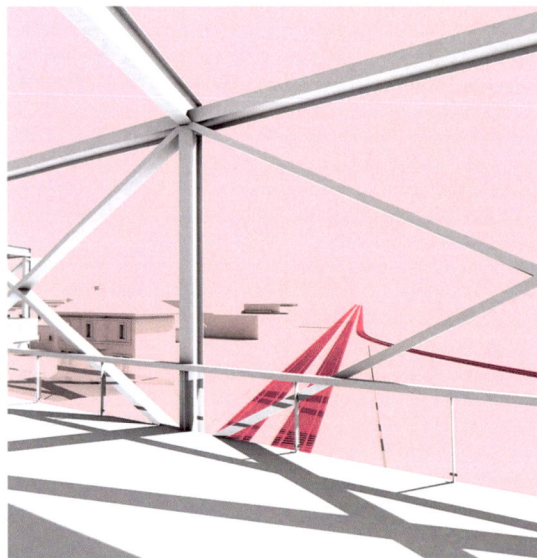

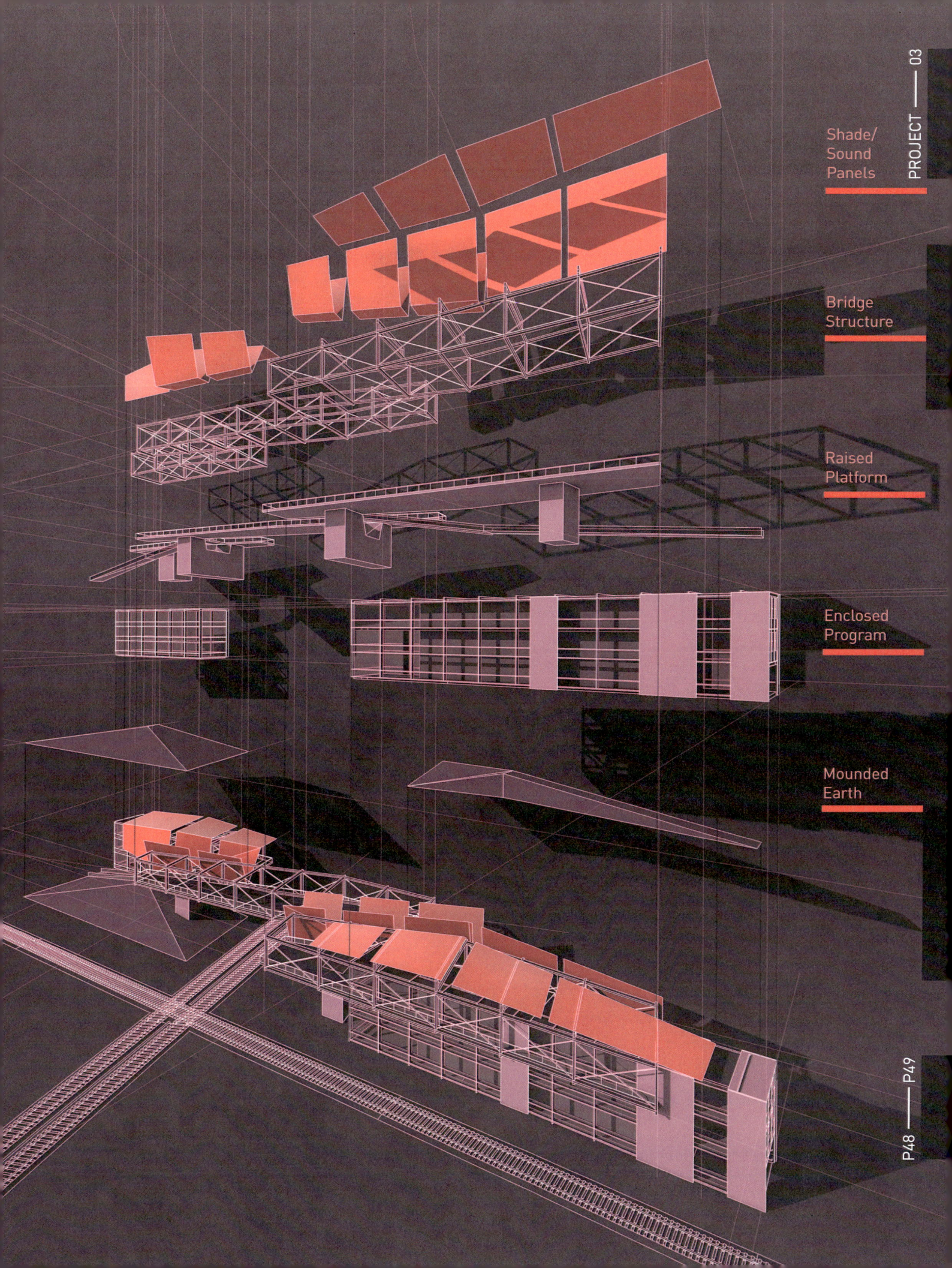

Shade/
Sound
Panels

Bridge
Structure

Raised
Platform

Enclosed
Program

Mounded
Earth

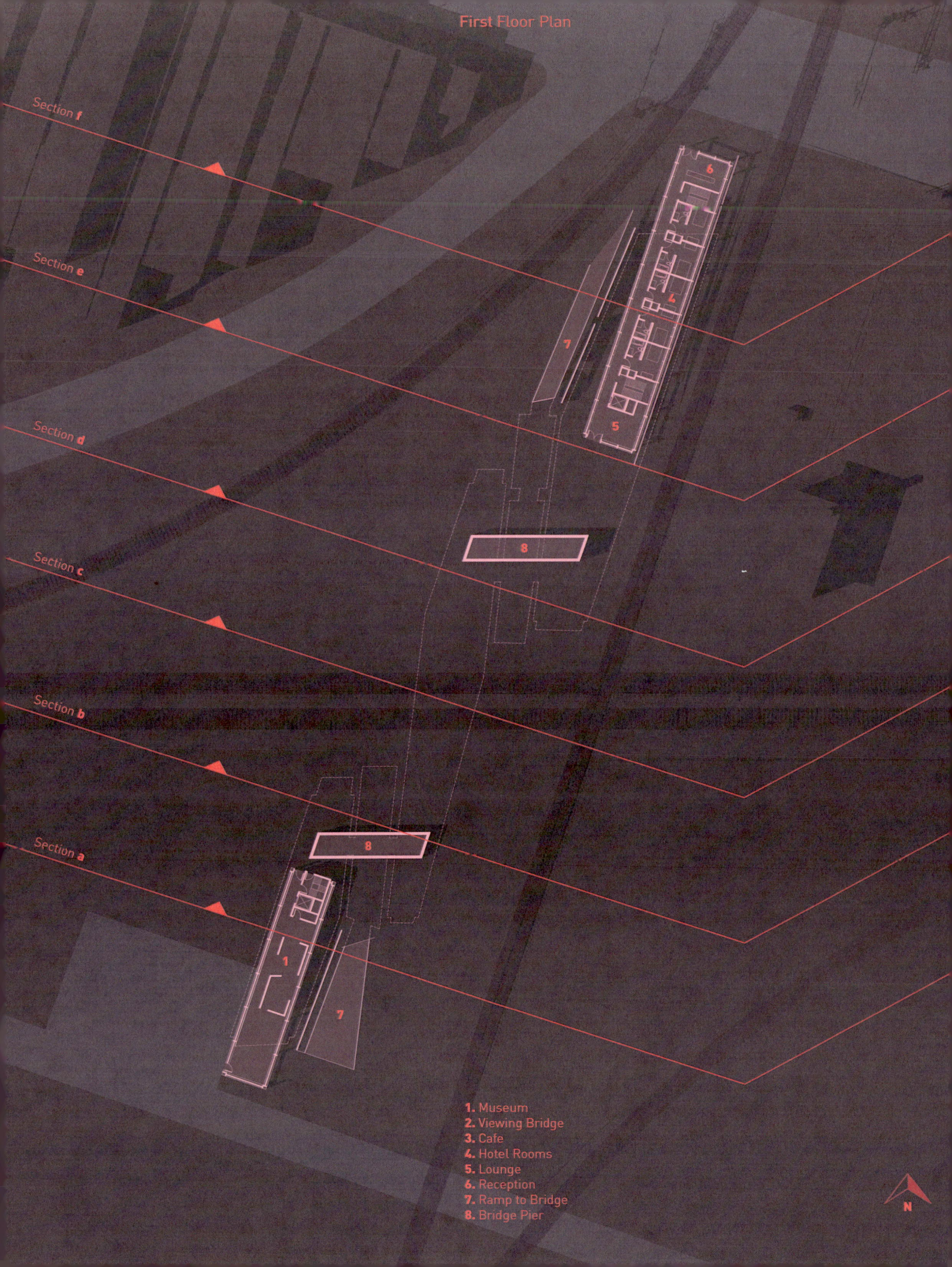

Section **f**

Section **e**

Section **d**

Section **c**

Section **b**

Section **a**

6

7

4

5

8

8

1

7

**1.** Museum
**2.** Viewing Bridge
**3.** Cafe
**4.** Hotel Rooms
**5.** Lounge
**6.** Reception
**7.** Ramp to Bridge
**8.** Bridge Pier

N

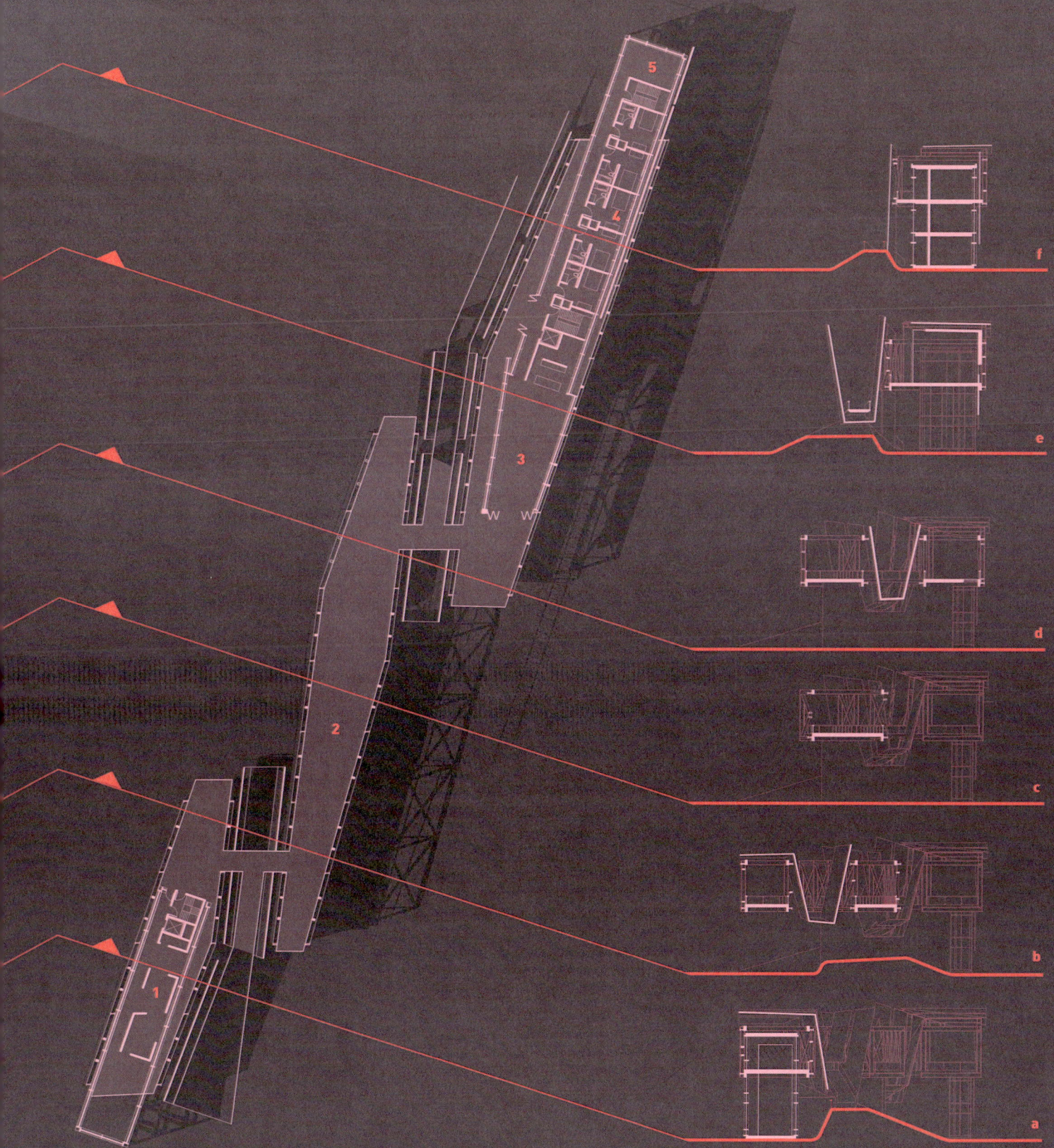

0'  10'  25'  50'  100'

## North Site Section

The scale of Main Street is small, limited to two and three floors. The new design mimics the lines and height of the existing buildings to continue the street edge fabric.

## East Site Section

While the new pavilion physically bridges over the east and west running tracks, it also bridges Main Street with the town's most important and historical feature- the crossroads. This connection facilitates interactions between visitors and residents, nearby restaurants, bars, and gift shops.

Main Street Architecture

Water Towers

Train Pavilion

Train Tracks

Train Pavilion

Main Street Architecture

Main Street Architecture

Grain Elevator

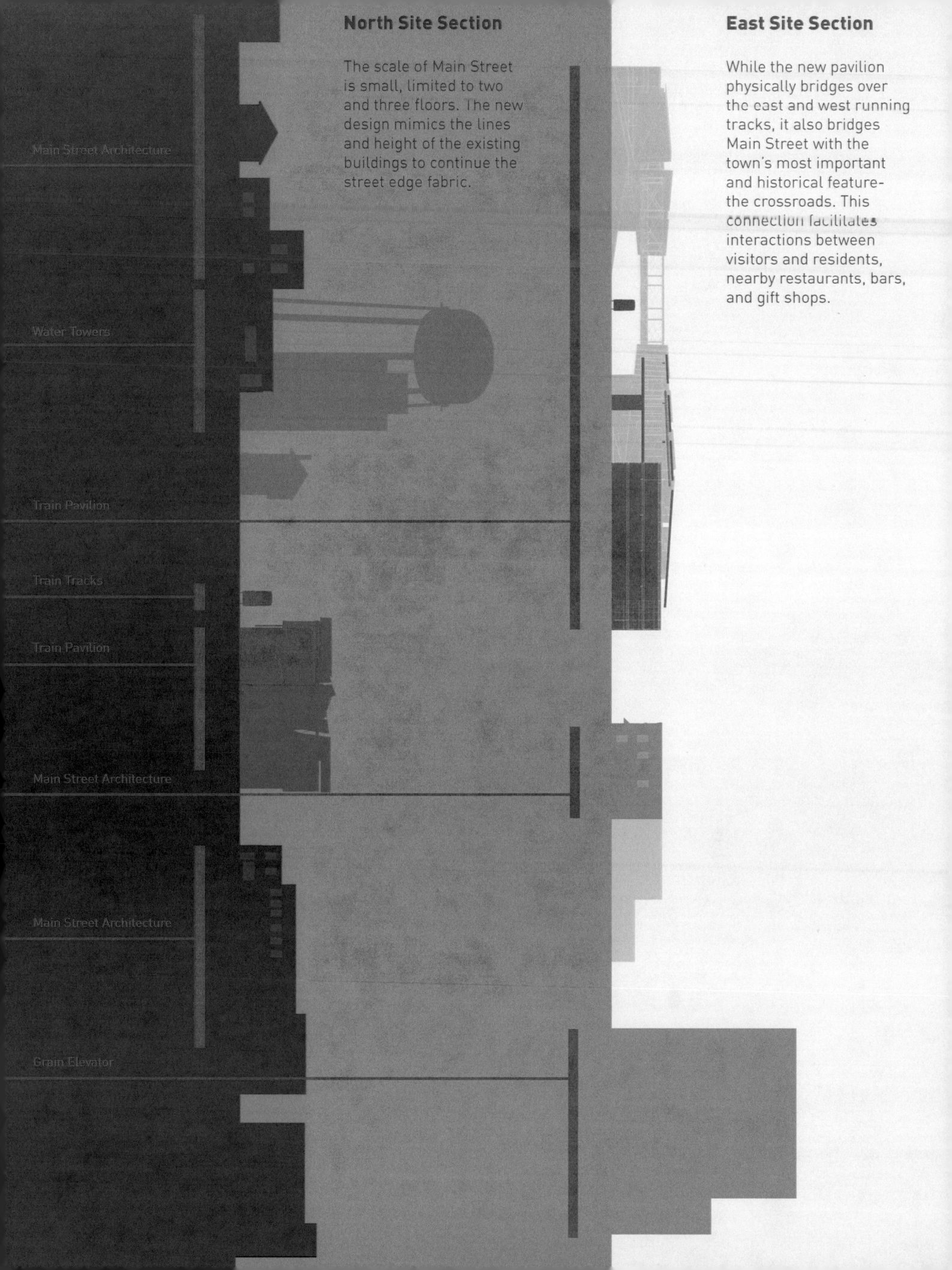

## West Elevation

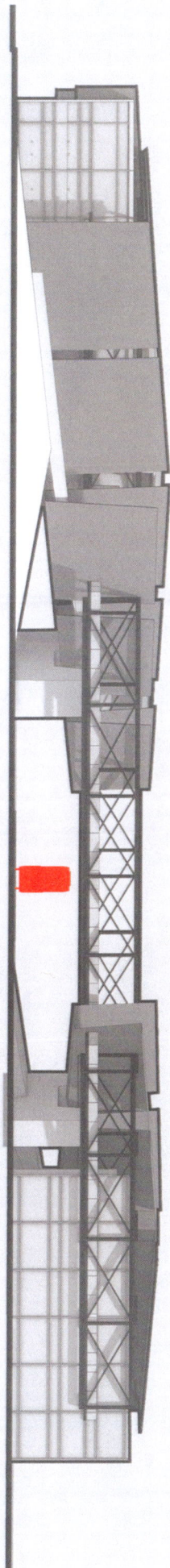

## East Elevation

Designed to place visitors as close to the trains as possible, the bridge fosters a heightened awareness of the railway's presence, as well as a place for social congregation. The bridge can be accessed directly from the ground by two large ramps or from the second floor hotel cafe and museum.

0'
10'
25'
50'

100'

## Interior Layering

The pavilion design places an open air cafe on the second floor adjacent to the bridge giving visitors one of the best places to view the town and passing trains as they dine. The structure wraps around the cafe suggesting slatted wooden box cars.

## Viewing Bridge

The surrounding landscape is designed as an informal and inviting experience. Much of the site appears desolate and run down due to years of neglect and heavy railroad use. Local wild grasses are replanted and sculpted hillocks provide a better viewing experience from the ground level.

## Old and New Materials

A variety of masonry structures on nearby Main Street provide a referential material palette. Materials chosen for the new pavilion hybridize the Main Street and industrial aesthetic, adding COR-TEN and black painted steel as primary materials. These materials relate to the historic structures of the nearby water tower and coal chute as well as the railways.

## Town Identity

The Village of Deshler has an important and distinct resource directly in its backyard. The new pavilion design clarifies the town's identity as a destination for train enthusiasts and acts as a social condenser through its unique siting and programmatic uses. This new focus can unite the town vision reversing the destruction of the existing Main Street fabric and landscape and instead bring a heightened awareness to it through an innovative form of historic preservation.

# CLIFF RETREAT

| | |
|---|---|
| **Project:** | Meditation Retreat |
| **Location:** | East Iceland |
| **Date:** | March 15, 2016 |

## 04

Iceland is known for its stunningly grand cliffs and the site of the cliff retreat is no exception. Situated on the west coast near Selárdalur, the design explores a dialect with the landscape. The retreat does not simply drop a structure onto the cliff, but instead engages the landscape by calling on inspiration from the surrounding landforms while providing stunning views.

Site Location

Iceland

175 miles

250 miles

Selárdalur

North
Atlantic
Ocean

West Shore

West Shore

3,500 ft

1,000 ft

## 1. Cliff Slit

An incision is made into the landscape and slopes towards the cliff edge.

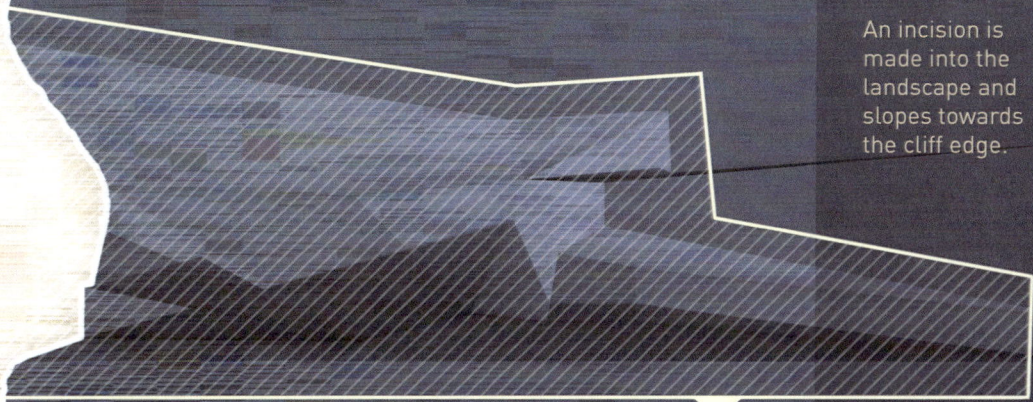

New Cliff Slit

## 2. Attachment

A light attachment to the landform allows water and landscape to flow around and under the structure.

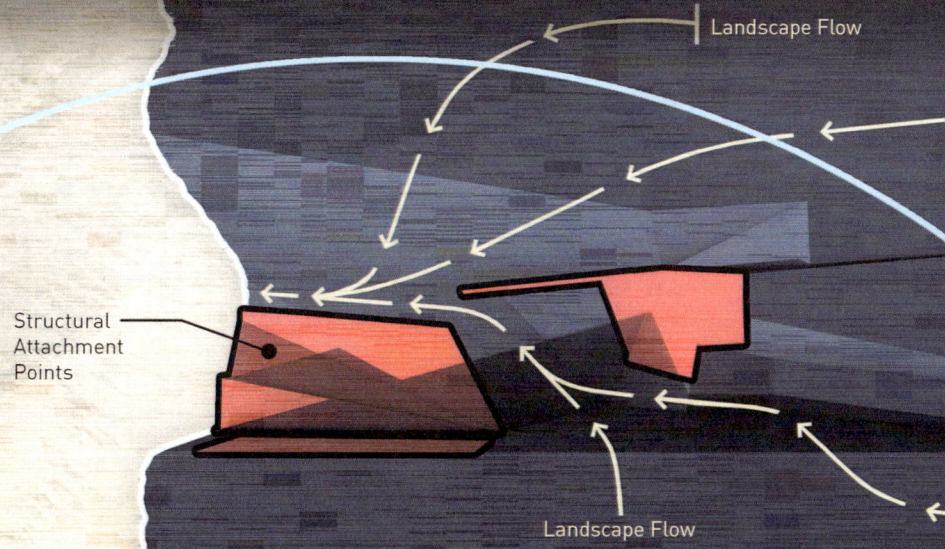

Landscape Flow

Structural Attachment Points

Landscape Flow

200 ft

100 ft

## 3. Architecture Overlay

A series of cantilevers and bridges open up and receive the landscape, creating sublime and intimate views from within.

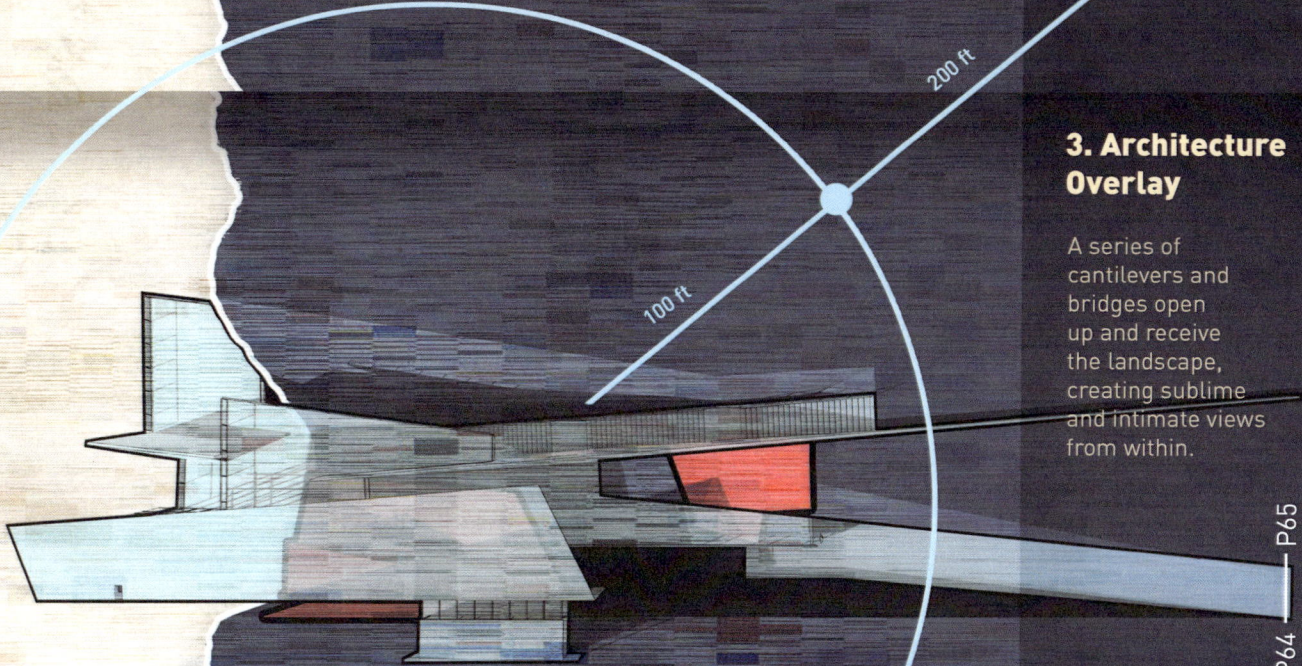

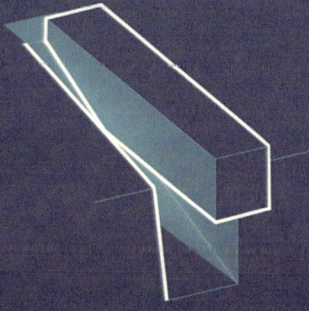

**Bridge**

1a

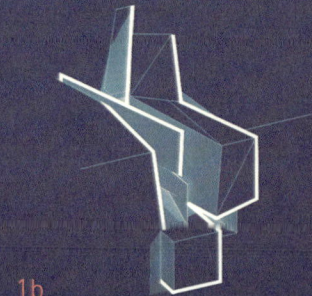

1b

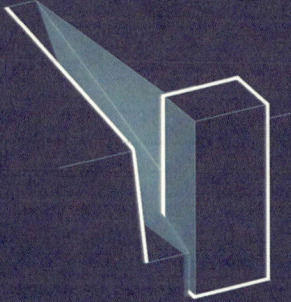

**Vertical**

2a

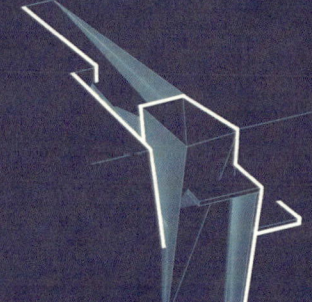

2b

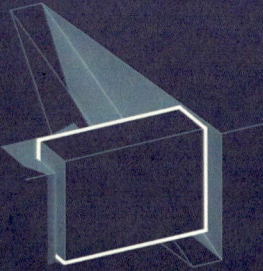

**Exposed**

3a

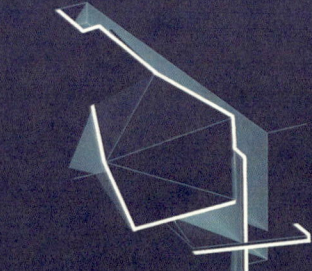

3b

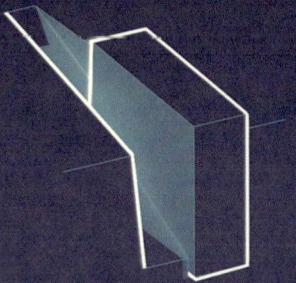

**Slot**

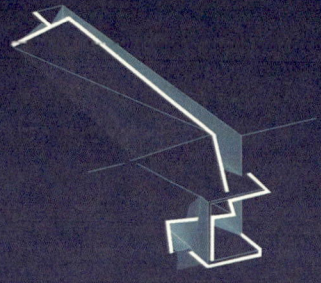

4a

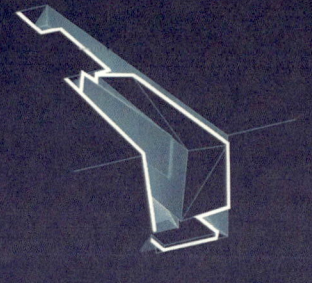

4b

## Form Iterations

Several strategies were explored to determine the best way to insert and orient the architecture. Ultimately, a hybrid of slot and bridge types were chosen to minimize visibility from the ocean as well as limit connection points to the cliff. This also allows for an abundance of landscape to proliferate around and below the design.

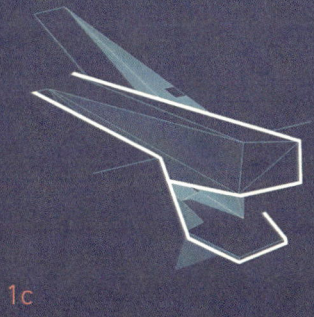

1c

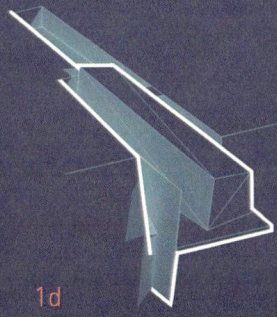

1d

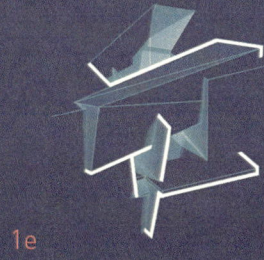

1e

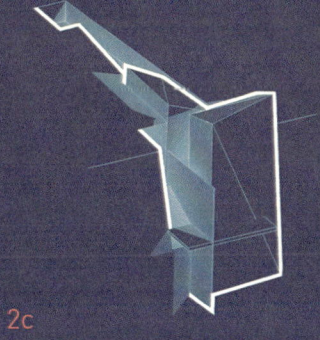

2c

2d

2e

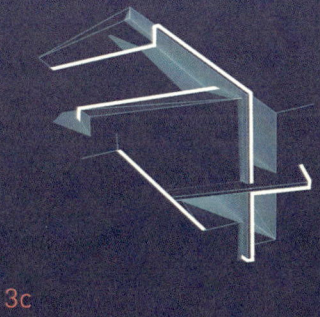

3c

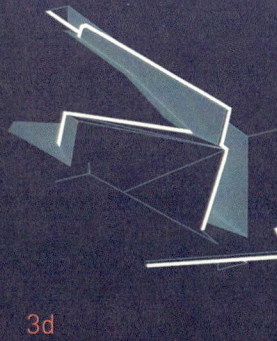

3d

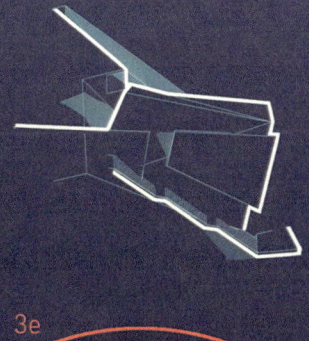

3e

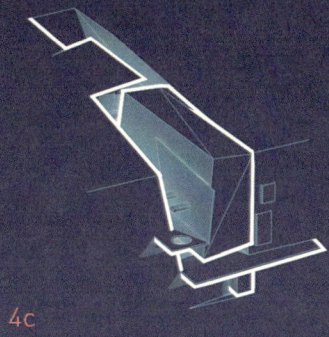

4c

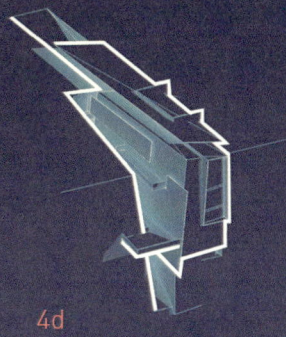

4d

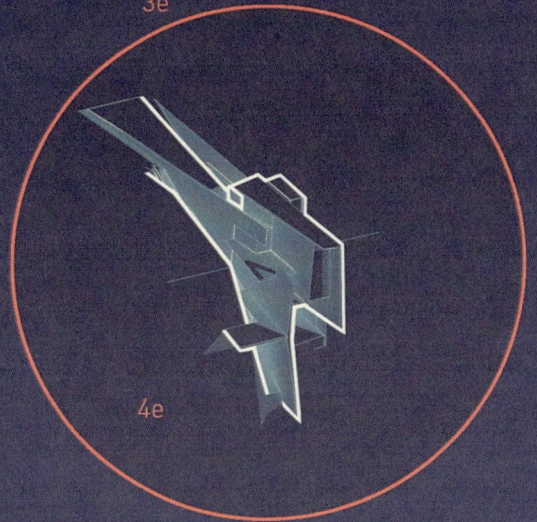

4e

Living Room

Dining

## Community to Meditative

The retreat program reflects a transition from public to private as one moves up and down the floors. The upper floors encourage interaction with large open floor plans and several places to congregate including the kitchen and lounges. These floors also serve as multipurpose rooms for nearby communities. The lower rooms gradually become more private, allowing for more private activities like sleeping and reading. The bottom floor opens back up to the outside with quiet meditative spaces and access to the lower gardens.

Grand Stair

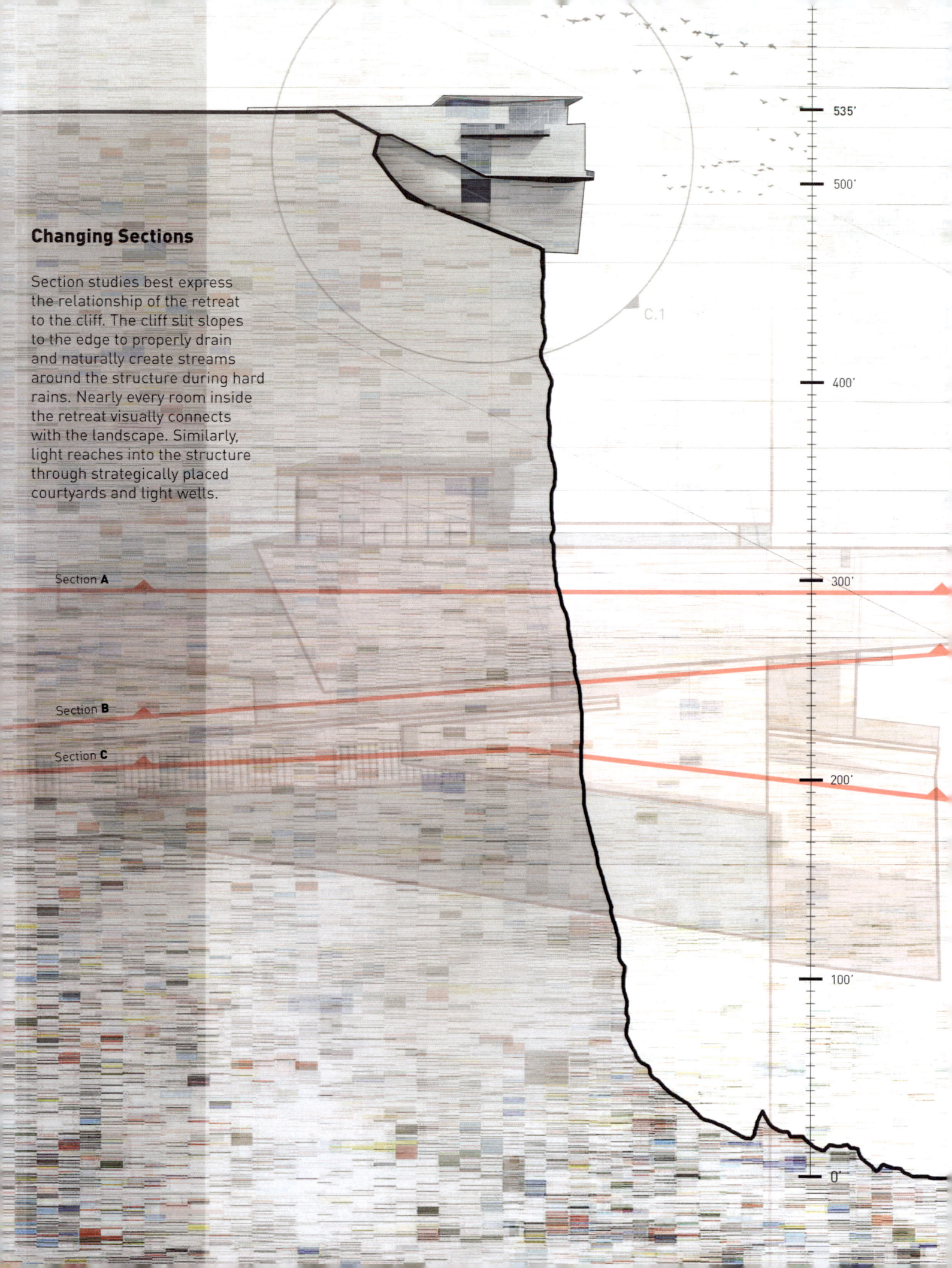

## Changing Sections

Section studies best express
the relationship of the retreat
to the cliff. The cliff slit slopes
to the edge to properly drain
and naturally create streams
around the structure during hard
rains. Nearly every room inside
the retreat visually connects
with the landscape. Similarly,
light reaches into the structure
through strategically placed
courtyards and light wells.

C.1

Section **A**

Section **B**

Section **C**

535'

500'

400'

300'

200'

100'

0'

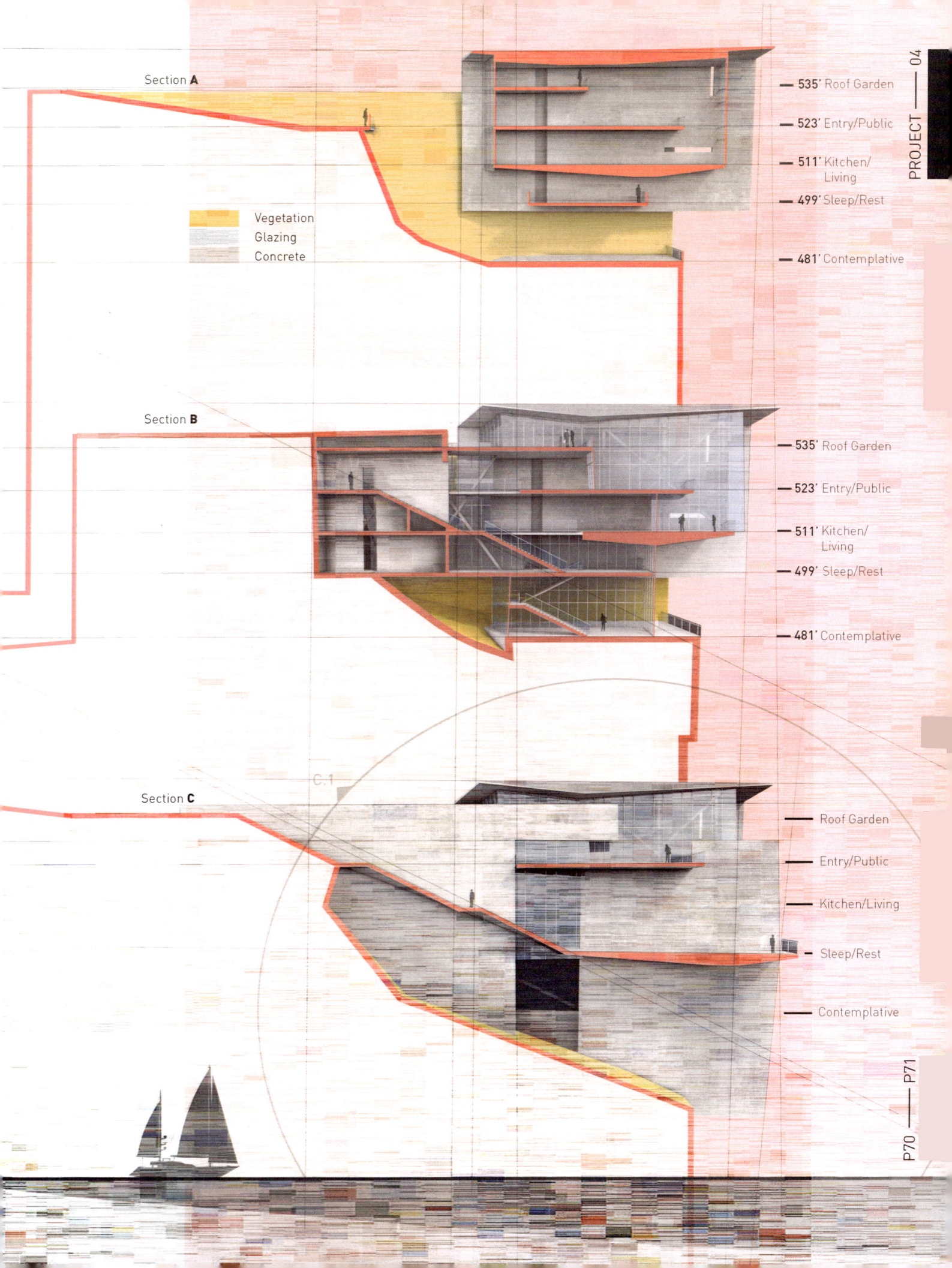

Section **A**

Vegetation
Glazing
Concrete

— 535' Roof Garden

— 523' Entry/Public

— 511' Kitchen/
Living

— 499' Sleep/Rest

— 481' Contemplative

Section **B**

— 535' Roof Garden

— 523' Entry/Public

— 511' Kitchen/
Living

— 499' Sleep/Rest

— 481' Contemplative

C.1

Section **C**

— Roof Garden

— Entry/Public

— Kitchen/Living

— Sleep/Rest

— Contemplative

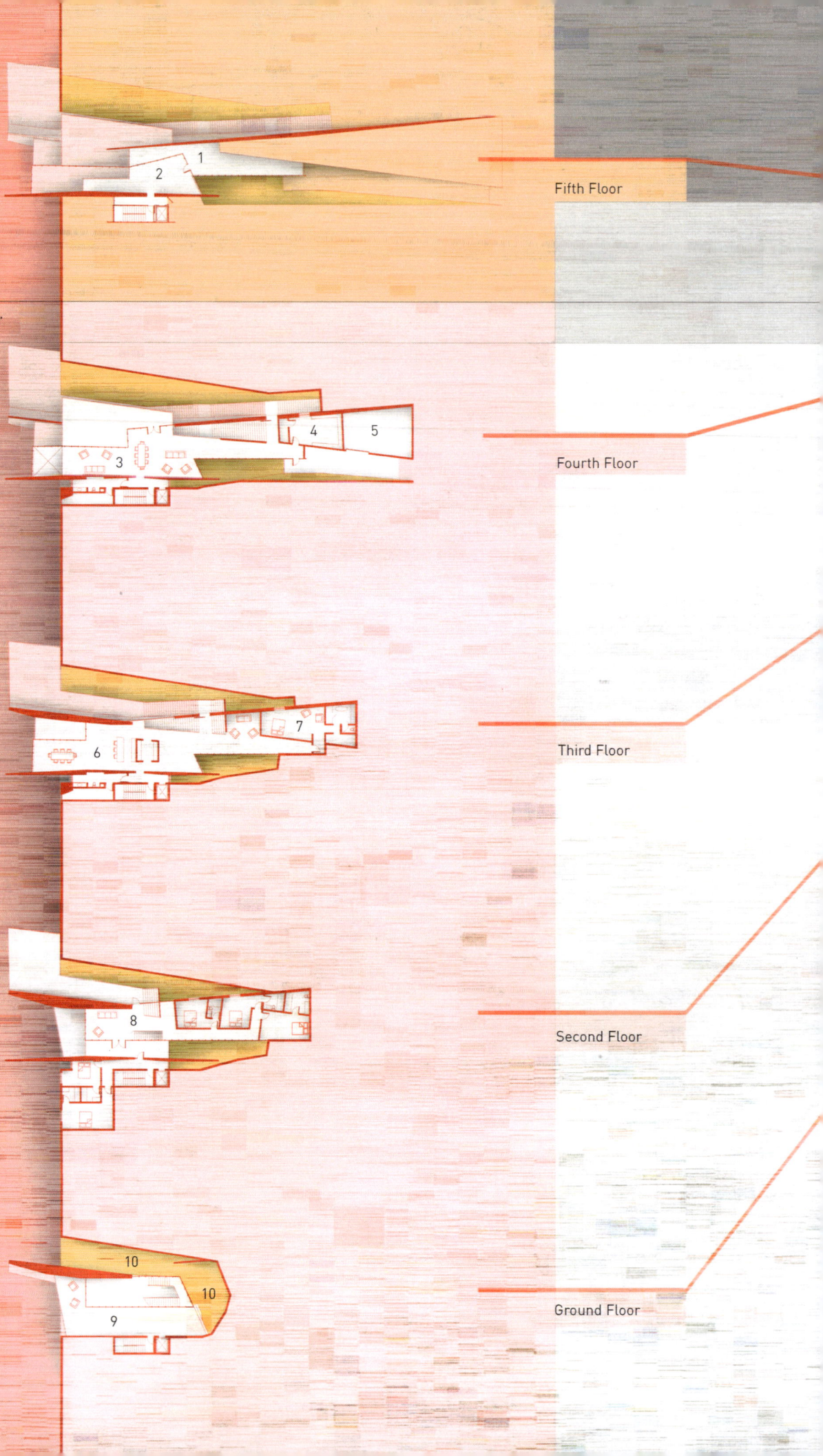

1. Roof Deck
2. Meditation
3. Community Room
4. Study
5. Storage
6. Kitchen/Dining
7. Bedroom
8. Sleeping Quarters
9. Lower Deck
10. Garden

100'    50'    25'  10'  0'

N

1

2

Fifth Floor

3

4

5

Fourth Floor

6

7

Third Floor

8

Second Floor

10

10

9

Ground Floor

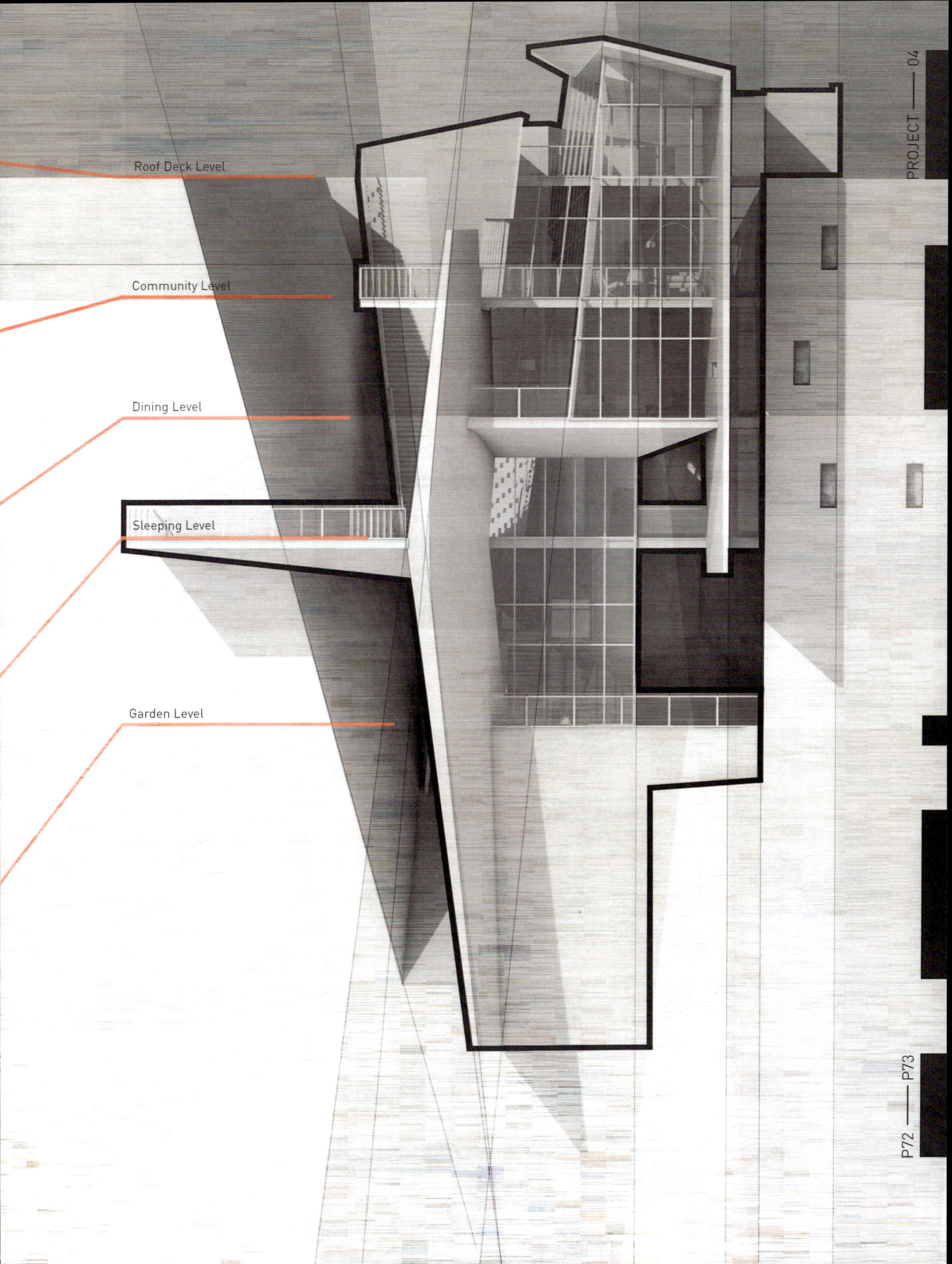

Roof Deck Level

Community Level

Dining Level

Sleeping Level

Garden Level

Cliff Cantilever

Bridge

Lookout

# Image Index

In order to better understand the development of the graphics seen in this portfolio, many illustrations are broken down to their most basic components. The following pages will provide insight into the software used, a preview of the 3D model, a preview of the base renderings, and the amount of Photoshop that went into each illustration.

## Foggy
## Wharf

P 10

Sketchup Model / Line Work

V-Ray Base Rendering

Photoshop Context,Sky, & Entourage

Photoshop Fog and Color

## Site
## Diagram

P 13

Sketchup Model / Line Work

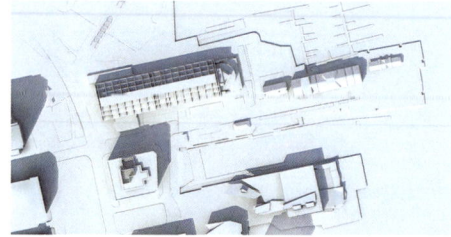

V-Ray Base Rendering

Photoshop Aerial Overlay

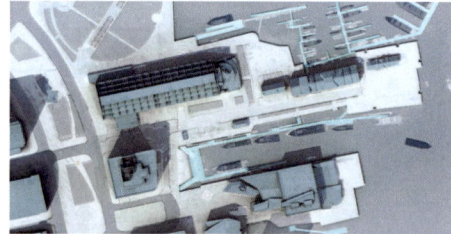

Photoshop Color

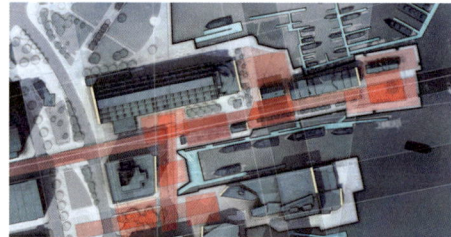

Photoshop Texture Overlay

## Line Work
## Study

P 16

Sketchup Model / Line Work

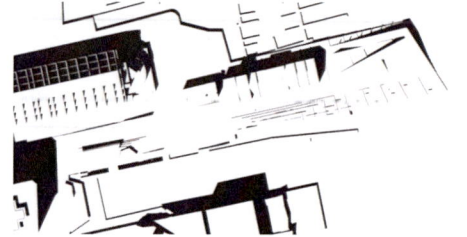

Sketchup Shadow

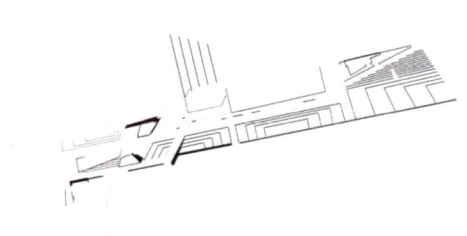

Photoshop Painted Line Work

Photoshop Painted Line Work

Photoshop Compiled Layers

# High-Res
# Site Plan

P 18

# Wharf
# Viewing

P 22

# Vessel
# Viewing

P 24

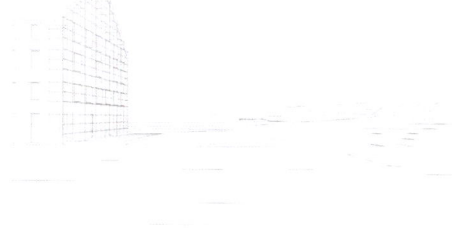

Sketchup Model / Line Work

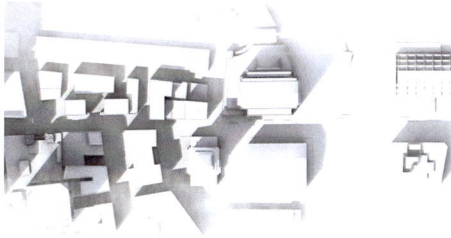

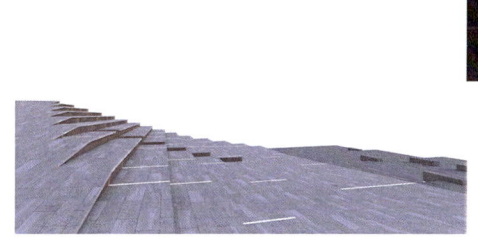

Sketchup Model / Line Work

Sketchup Model / Line Work

V-Ray Base Rendering

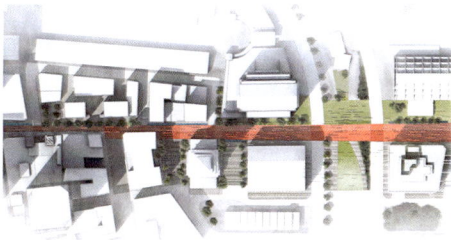

V-Ray Base Rendering

V-Ray Base Rendering

Photoshop Color & Texture

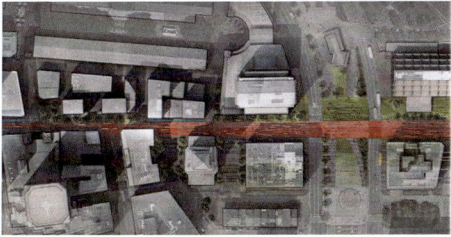

Photoshop Context, Sky, & Entourage

Photoshop Context and Sky

Photoshop Aerial Overlay

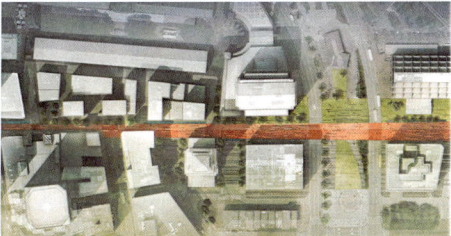

Photoshop Edge Masking

Photoshop Grass, Lights, and People

Photoshop Color and Atmosphere

Photoshop Color Adjustments

## Vintage
## Perspective

P 28

Sketchup Model / Line Work

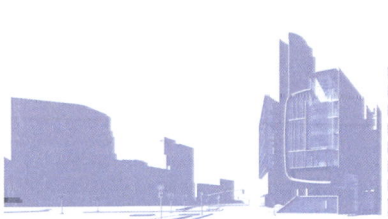

Sketchup Colorized Shadows

V-Ray Clay Rendering Overlay

Photoshop Color Overlay

Photoshop Entourage, Trees, and Sky

## Concept
## Diagram

P 32

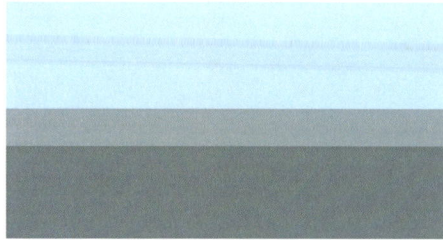

Photoshop Color Base

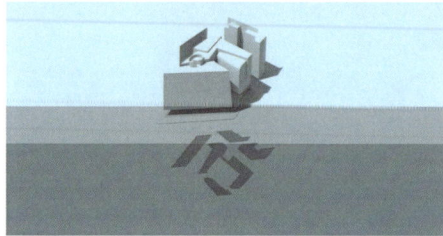

V-Ray Clay Rendering

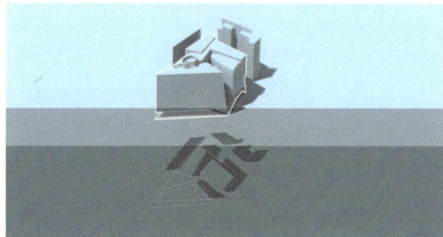

Photoshop Profile Line Work

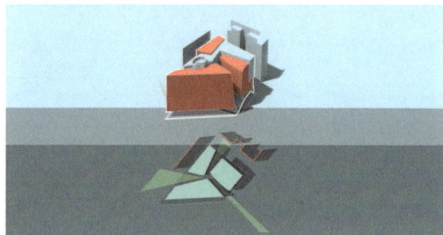

Photoshop Color Overlay

## Perspective
## Site Plan

P 34

Sketchup Model / Line Work

V-Ray Base Rendering

Photoshop Textures

Photoshop / Topaz Coloring

## Daytime
## Nighttime

P 36

## Simple
## Elevation

P 38

## Snow
## Bird's Eye

P 40

Sketchup Model / Line Work

Sketchup Model / Line Work

Sketchup Model / Line Work

V-Ray Base Rendering

V-Ray Clay Rendering

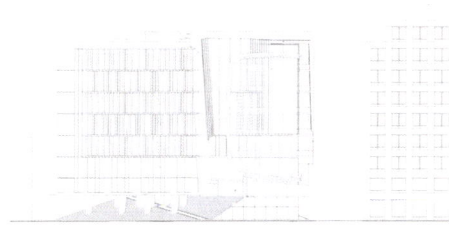

V-Ray Base Rendering

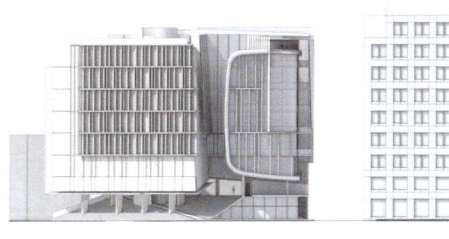

Photoshop Context, Entourage, and Vegetation

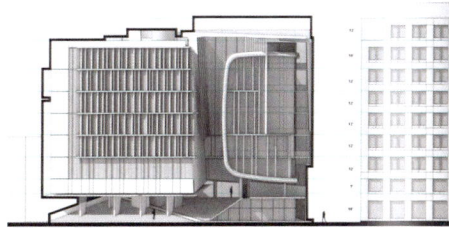

Photoshop Profile and Shading

V-Ray Clay Rendering

Photoshop / Topaz Atmosphere and Coloring

Photoshop Textures and Vegetation

Photoshop Night Editing

Photoshop Fog / Topaz Coloring

## Aerial
## Diagram

P 44

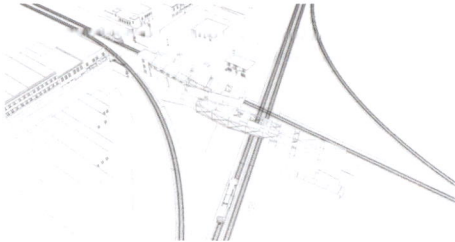

Sketchup Model / Line Work

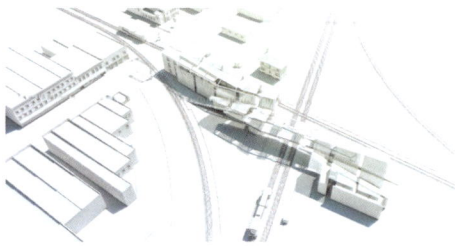

V-Ray Clay Rendering

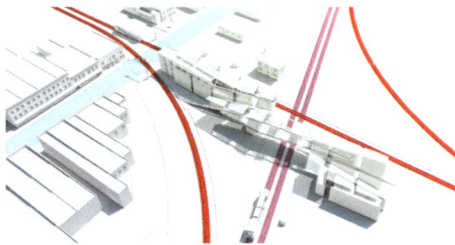

Photoshop Color Overlay

## View
## Diagram

P 47

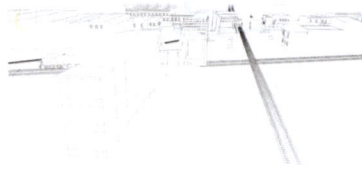

Sketchup Model / Line Work

V-Ray Clay Rendering

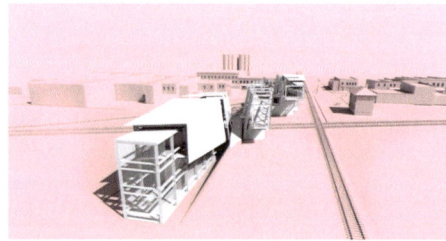

Photoshop Background Color

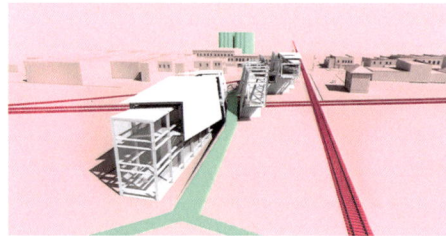

Photoshop Detail Color

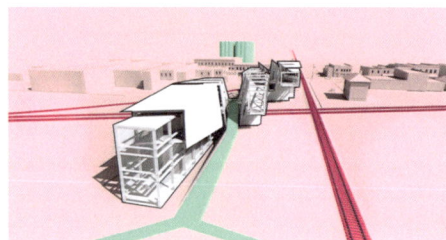

Photoshop Outline

## Exploded
## Axon

P 49

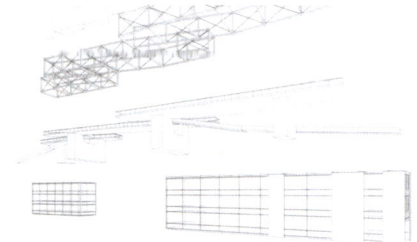

Sketchup Model / Line Work

V-Ray Clay Rendering

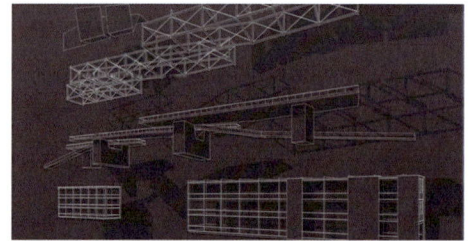

Photoshop Color Invert

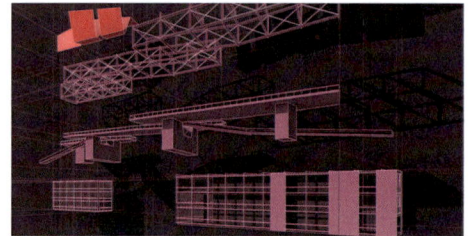

Photoshop Coloring

## Floor
## Plans

P 50

## Interior
## Perspective

P 54

## Exterior
## Vignette

P 55

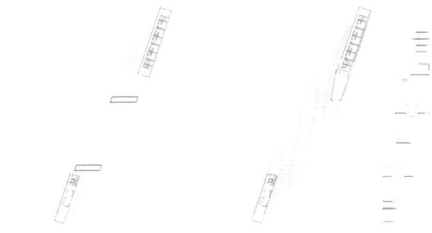

Sketchup Model / Line Work

Sketchup Model / Line Work

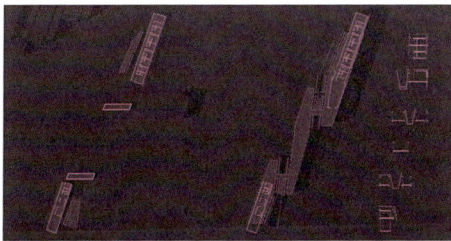

Sketchup Model / Line Work

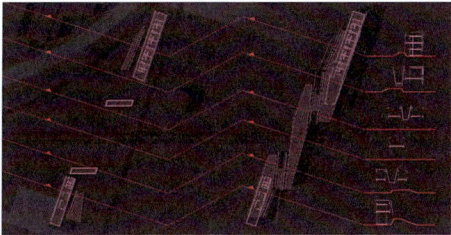

Sketchup Shadow

V-Ray Base Rendering

V-Ray Base Rendering

Photoshop Coloring

Photoshop People and Context

Photoshop Landscape, People, and Sky

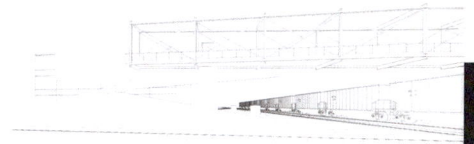

Photoshop Detail

Photoshop Lights

Photoshop Color and Atmosphere

Photoshop Coloring / Topaz

# Main St.
# Perspective

P 56

V-Ray Clay Rendering

V-Ray Base Rendering

Photoshop Context and Sky

Photoshop People and Details

Photoshop Lighting / Topaz Coloring

# Pavilion
# Aerial

P 58

Sketchup Model / Line Work

V-Ray Base Rendering

Photoshop Context and Light

Photoshop Color and Atmosphere

# Cliff
# Vignette

P 62

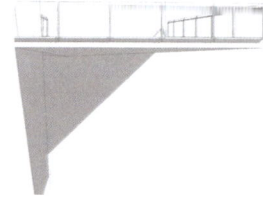

Sketchup Model / Line Work

V-Ray Clay Rendering

Photoshop Context and Sky

Photoshop Textures

Photoshop Color and Topaz

## Cliff Cut
## Diagram

P 65

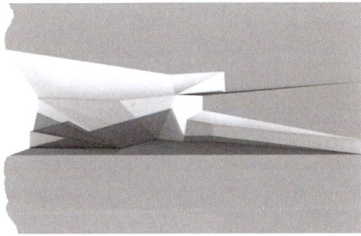

V-Ray Clay Rendering

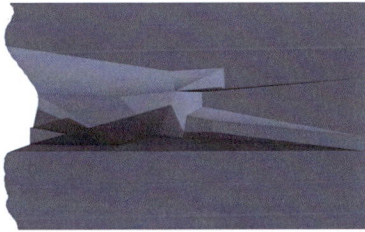

Photoshop Color

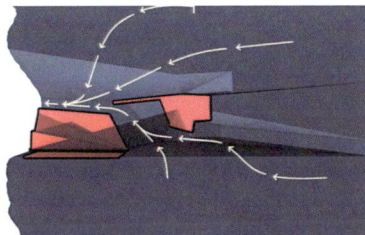

Photoshop Color and Arrows

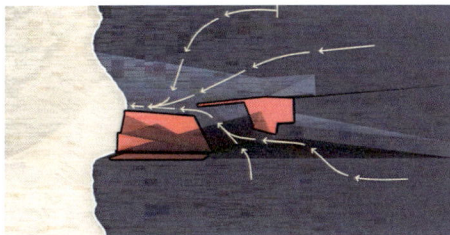

Photoshop Texture

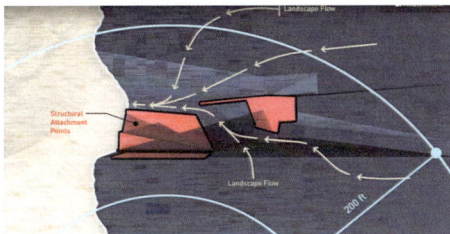

Photoshop Annotation

## Form Study
## Iterations

P 66

Sketchup Model / Line Work

V-Ray Clay Rendering

Photoshop Profile Outline

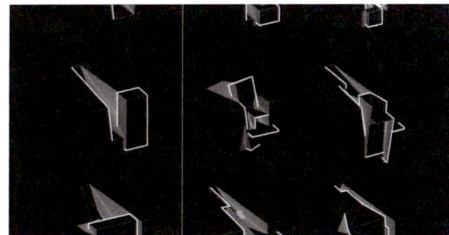

Photoshop Color Invert

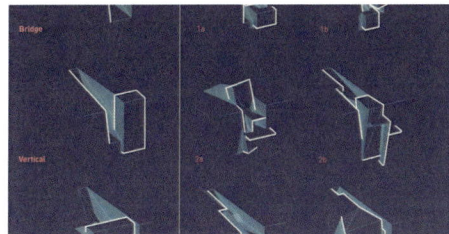

Photoshop Color and Annotation

## Retreat
## Interior

P 68

Sketchup Model / Line Work

V-Ray Base Rendering

Photoshop Black and White

Photoshop People, Vegetation, and Lights

## Building
## Section

P 70

Sketchup Model / Line Work

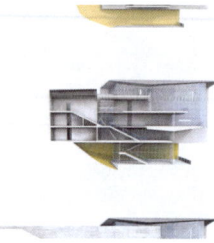

V-Ray Base Rendering

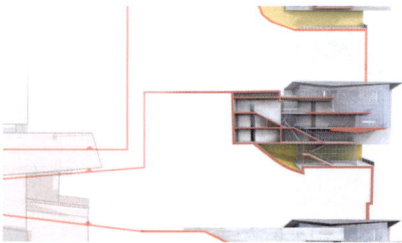

Photoshop Cut Poche

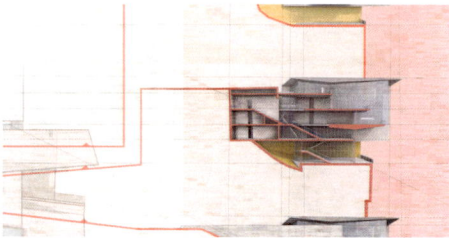

Photoshop Color and Textures

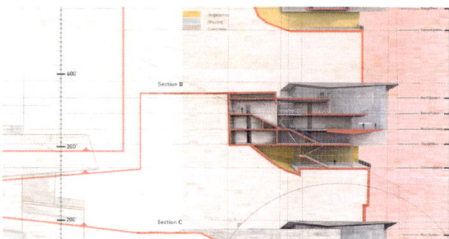

Photoshop Annotation

## Exterior
## Vignette 1

P 74

Sketchup Model / Line Work

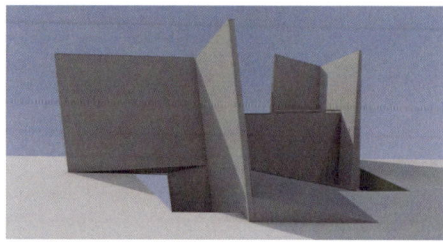

V-Ray Base Rendering

Photoshop Texture

Photoshop Atmosphere and BW

## Exterior
## Vignette 2

P 74

Sketchup Model / Line Work

V-Ray Base Rendering

Photoshop Texture

Photoshop Atmosphere and BW

## Unique Perspectives

Ultimately, the architecture acts as
a backdrop to the environment that
surrounds it. The grandness of the cliff
edge and energy of the waves crashing
below allows the architecture to frame an
experience, rather than dominate it.

# Exterior
# Vignette 3

P 75

# Cliff
# Aerial

P 76

Sketchup Model / Line Work

Sketchup Model

V-Ray Base Rendering

V-Ray Base Rendering

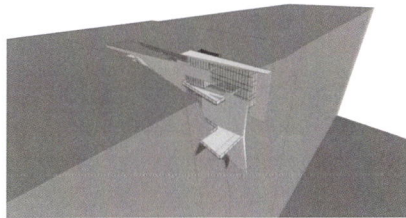

Photoshop Texture

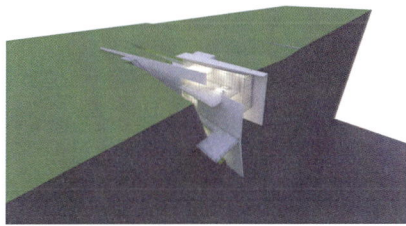

Photoshop Landscape Textures

Photoshop Atmosphere and BW

Photoshop Darken and Color

Photoshop Color and Topaz

www.**visualizing**architecture.com

www.ingramcontent.com/pod-product-compliance
Lightning Source LLC
Chambersburg PA
CBRC100736150426
42811CB00070B/1914

9 780099 138293